Teaching Pal ①

Authors and Advisors

Alma Flor Ada • Kylene Beers • F. Isabel Campoy
Joyce Armstrong Carroll • Nathan Clemens
Anne Cunningham • Martha Hougen
Elena Izquierdo • Carol Jago • Erik Palmer
Robert Probst • Shane Templeton • Julie Washington

Contributing Consultants

David Dockterman • Mindset Works
Jill Eggleton

Navigating the Teaching Pal

The Teaching Pal is a companion to the Teacher's Guide, providing point-of-use instructional notes for using the student texts in *my*Book for different purposes.

Blue Notes
READ FOR UNDERSTANDING

During a first reading of the complete text, use these notes to guide collaborative discussion about the gist of the text.

 READ FOR UNDERSTANDING

ASK: Why is Dilly alone? *(Possible responses: Minna could not swim as fast as Dilly; Dilly was having so much fun, he didn't think about where he was going.)*

ANNOTATION TIP: Have children underline the words that tell how Dilly feels.

FOLLOW-UP: What do you think Dilly will do? *(Accept reasonable responses.)*

DOK 2

Purple Notes
TARGETED CLOSE READ

During subsequent readings, use these notes to take a closer look at sections of the text to apply a reading skill.

 TARGETED CLOSE READ

Characters

Have children reread pages 70–71 to identify the story characters.

ASK: Who are the characters in the story? *(two friends, Dilly and Minna)*

FOLLOW-UP: What do you know about them? *(Dilly looks different from Minna and the other ducks; Dilly and Minna like to have fun together.)*

ANNOTATION TIP: Have children underline the words that describe Dilly.

DOK 3

Yellow Notes

Use these notes for teaching support on the pages that appear before and after each text.

Academic Discussion

Use the TURN AND TALK routine. Remind children to follow agreed-upon rules for discussion, such as taking turns speaking and adding to their partner's ideas.

Possible responses:

- Why was Dilly bigger than the other ducks? Would Dilly ever see Minna again? DOK 1
- Even though Dilly looks different, he is still special. DOK 2

Red Notes
NOTICE & NOTE

Use these notes to help children learn to look for signposts in a text in order to create meaning.

Notice & Note

Contrasts and Contradictions

Remind children that when a character acts or feels differently than we expect, the author is showing us something important about the character.

Tell them that when that happens, they should stop to notice and note, which includes asking themselves questions about what they read.

Have children explain why they might use this strategy on pages 72–73. *(Dilly was always happy, but now he is sad and afraid.)*

Remind them of the Anchor Question: **Why might Dilly feel this way?** *(He is alone and lost.)*

DOK 2

TABLE OF CONTENTS

4

5

MODULE 2

My Family, My Community

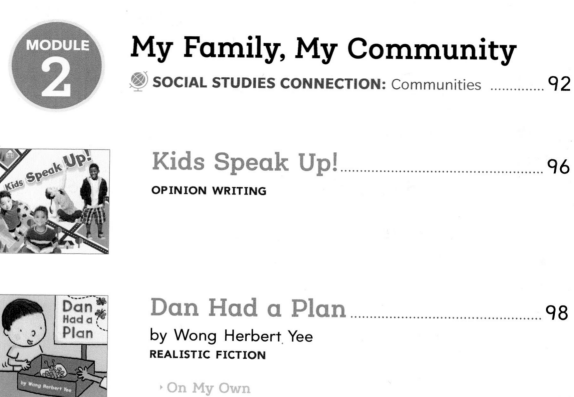

Introduce the Topic

- **Read aloud** the module title, *Nice to Meet You!*
- **Tell children** that in this module they will be reading texts about the topic of new friends and experiences.
- **Have children** share prior knowledge about the topic or word associations for new friends and experiences. Record their ideas in a web.

Discuss the Quotation

- **Read aloud** the quotation.
- **Lead a discussion** in which children try to explain the quote in their own words. Explain the meaning, as needed: *It's exciting to make new friends, but we also appreciate and enjoy the friends we already have. Silver and gold are both valuable, just like old friends and new friends.*

ASK: What are some ways that you can make a new friend? *(Accept reasonable responses.)*

MODULE
1

Nice to Meet You!

"Make new friends, but keep the old.
One is silver, the other gold."

—Traditional Song

8

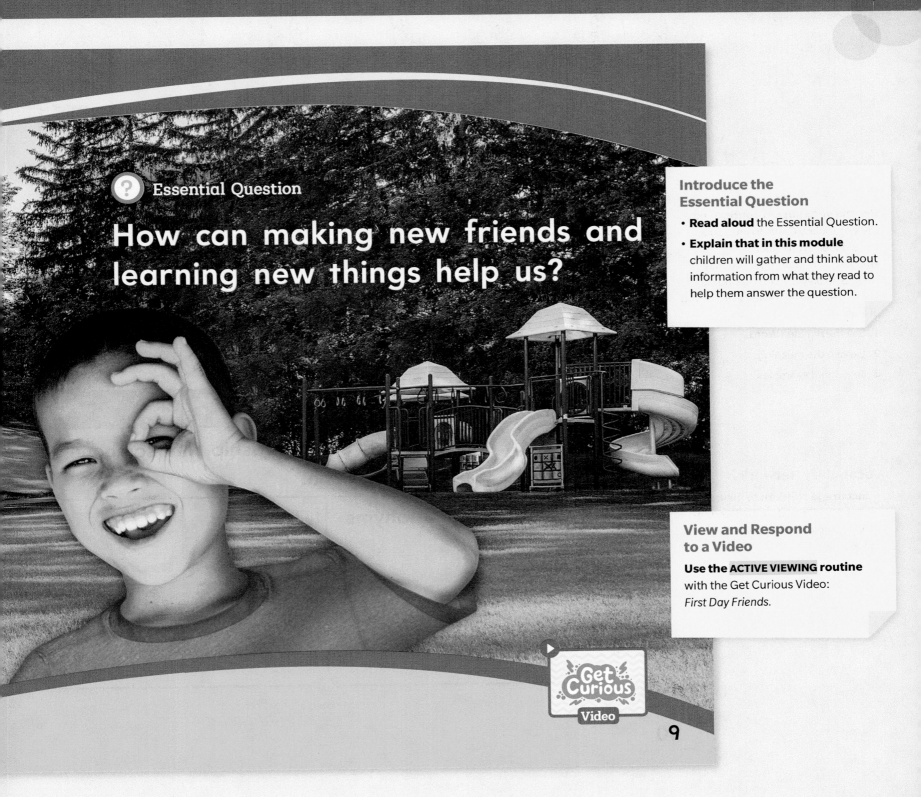

? Essential Question

How can making new friends and learning new things help us?

Introduce the Essential Question

- **Read aloud** the Essential Question.
- **Explain that in this module** children will gather and think about information from what they read to help them answer the question.

View and Respond to a Video

Use the ACTIVE VIEWING routine with the Get Curious Video: *First Day Friends.*

Get Curious Video

Big Idea Words

Use the VOCABULARY routine and the Vocabulary Cards to introduce the Big Idea Words *friendship, emotions,* and *challenge.* You may wish to display the corresponding Vocabulary Card for each word as you discuss it.

1. Say the Big Idea Word.

2. Explain the meaning.

3. Talk about examples.

Vocabulary Network

- **Encourage children** to think about what they like to do with friends as they complete the activity for *friendship*.

Words About New Friends and Experiences

Complete the Vocabulary Network to show what you know about the words.

friendship

Meaning: When you have a **friendship** with someone, you like the person.

Synonyms and Antonyms	Drawing

emotions

Meaning: **Emotions** are strong feelings we have, like happiness or sadness.

Synonyms and Antonyms	Drawing

challenge

Meaning: A **challenge** is something that is hard to do.

Synonyms and Antonyms	Drawing

Vocabulary Network

- **As children complete** the activity for *emotions*, prompt them to think of different kinds of feelings they can have.

- **Ask children** to think about a *challenge* they might face in school and a *challenge* they might face outside of school.

READ FOR UNDERSTANDING

Introduce the Text

Read aloud the title, *My First Day*. Tell children that this story is realistic fiction. Explain that realistic fiction stories are made up but could happen in real life. Their characters are like real people, the settings look like real places, and the events could really happen.

• Guide children to **set a purpose.**

• **Read the text** with children.

DOK 3

 READ FOR UNDERSTANDING

Story Structure

ASK: What was the girl busy doing on her first day of school? (*Possible responses: singing songs; reading books; having fun on the swings*)

FOLLOW-UP: How do you know? (*The pictures inside the heart tell what she did on her first day of school.*)

DOK 2

My First Day

my writing ideas

It was my first day of school!
There was so much to do!

12

First, we sang.

Next, we listened to a story.
I did all my work.

Then, we played.
It was fun!

Last, we said goodbye.
See you tomorrow!

13

📖 **READ FOR UNDERSTANDING**

Story Structure

ASK: What happens at the beginning, middle, and end of the story? (*The kids sing at the beginning; they listen to a story, do work, and play in the middle; they leave school at the end.*)

FOLLOW-UP: How do you know the order in which the events happen in the story? (*Possible responses: The story is told in order; the words first, next, then, and last tell the order in which the events happen.*)

ANNOTATION TIP: Have children circle the words that signal the order of events.

DOK 2

Guided Practice

READ Together

 READ FOR UNDERSTANDING

Introduce the Text

- **Read aloud** and discuss the information about the genre.
- **Guide children** to set a purpose for reading to practice asking and answering questions.
- **Provide information** about the author, Pam Muñoz Ryan.
- **Tell children** to look for and think about the Power Words as they read.

Prepare to Read

GENRE STUDY **Narrative nonfiction** gives information, but it sounds like a story. Look for:

- photos that show real people
- photos that show real places
- facts about a real topic

SET A PURPOSE **Ask questions** before, during, and after you read to help you get information or understand the text. Look for evidence in the text and pictures to **answer** the questions.

POWER WORDS
new
try
great
enjoy
excited
nervous

Meet Pam Muñoz Ryan.

14

Try This!

by Pam Muñoz Ryan

Ask and Answer Questions

MODEL ASKING AND ANSWERING A QUESTION

Q **THINK ALOUD** *As I read, I ask questions about things I don't understand, or things I want to learn more about. This text says that the children go to school. I ask myself: How do the children get to school? I'll look at the text and photos to see if they help me answer my question.*

DOK 2

We go to school.

16

This is new.
Try this, Sam!

17

READ FOR UNDERSTANDING

ASK: What is new for Sam? (*taking a bus to school*)

FOLLOW-UP: What clues in the text and photos help you know this? (*The text says this is new; the photo shows Sam getting on a school bus.*)

DOK 2

READ FOR UNDERSTANDING

Phonics/Decoding in Context

Have children point to the word *Sam*. Review that when a word has a consonant, followed by a vowel, followed by a consonant, the vowel usually stands for the short vowel sound. **Model blending** the sounds in the word: /s/ /ă/ /m/, *Sam*. Have children repeat. Point out that *Sam* is a name and names begin with a capital letter.

ANNOTATION TIP: Have children circle the letter that stands for the short *a* in *Sam*. Have them underline the capital letter.

Notice & Note

3 Big Questions

- **Remind children** that when they are reading nonfiction, they should stop and think about the 3 Big Questions:

- **What surprised me?** Tell children to pay attention to something they find interesting or something they learned.

- **What did the author think I already knew?** Have children note ideas that are confusing, or words that they don't know the meaning of.

- **What challenged, changed, or confirmed what I already knew?** Ask children to think about whether what they read confirmed or changed their thinking.

- **Have children** explain why they might ask themselves one or more of the 3 Big Questions on pages 18–19. (*Possible response: It surprised me that Sam made a friend on the bus. I didn't think he would on the first day because it took me a few days to make friends on the bus.*)

DOK 3

We like this bus.

This bus is great!

19

READ FOR UNDERSTANDING

Ask and Answer Questions

MODEL ASKING AND ANSWERING A QUESTION

🗨 **THINK ALOUD** *I wonder what the children do in their new rooms? I'll keep reading to see if I can find out the answer to my question.*

DOK 2

🔍 **TARGETED CLOSE READ**

Author's Purpose

Have children reread pages 20–21 to analyze the author's purpose.

ASK: What does this text tell about? *(new things kids can do at school)*

FOLLOW-UP: Why does the author tell about these new things? *(She wants to tell the reader what new things might happen on their first few days of school.)*

DOK 3

We go to new rooms.

20

📖 **READ FOR UNDERSTANDING**

ASK: What does Sam try to do on this page? *(He tries to paint a picture.)*

ANNOTATION TIP: Have children circle the part of the photo that helps them answer the question.

DOK 2

This is new.
Try to paint, Sam!

21

We go outside at school.

This is new.
Try to bat, Sam!

READ FOR UNDERSTANDING

Phonics/Decoding in Context

Have children point to the word *bat*. Review that when a word has a consonant, followed by a vowel, followed by a consonant, the vowel usually stands for its short vowel sound. **Model blending** the sounds in the word: /b/ /ă/ /t/, *bat*. Have children repeat.

ANNOTATION TIP: Have children circle the letter that stands for the short *a* sound in the word *bat*. Have them find and circle another word with the short *a* sound. *(Sam)*

23

TARGETED CLOSE READ

Author's Purpose

Have children reread page 24 to analyze the author's purpose.

ASK: Why did the author write this text? (*Possible response: to give facts about new things kids can do at school*)

FOLLOW-UP: What does the author want you to learn? (*that it is good to try new things*)

DOK 3

READ FOR UNDERSTANDING

Wrap Up

Revisit the predictions children made before reading. Have them confirm or correct their predictions using evidence from the text and pictures.

DOK 2

School is great!
We like to try.

Turn and Talk

Use details from **Try This!** to answer these questions with a partner.

1. **Ask and Answer Questions** What questions did you ask yourself about **Try This!** before, during, and after reading? How did your questions help you understand the text?

2. How does Sam feel at the end? Tell why.

 Listening Tip

Listen carefully. Look at your partner to show that you are paying attention.

Academic Discussion

Use the TURN AND TALK routine.
Remind children to follow agreed-upon rules for discussion, such as listening carefully and looking at their partner while he or she speaks.

Possible responses:

1. *What instrument is Sam playing? What is the girl making?* DOK 2

2. *Sam is happy because he tried many new things; Sam learned that he likes doing new things.* DOK 2

DOK 3

25

Write a Caption

PROMPT Look back at **Try This!** What new things does Sam try to do?

PLAN First, draw a picture of something new Sam does.

WRITE Now write a sentence to be a caption for your picture. Tell about the new thing Sam does. Use this for help:

Sam can _____.

Remember to:

- Begin with a capital letter.
- End with a period.

Responses may vary.

Write About Reading
- **Read aloud** the Write section.
- **Help children** write a simple sentence that includes a subject and a verb. Encourage them to begin their sentences with a capital letter and end them with a period.

DOK 3

27

Independent Close Reading

Have children close read and annotate "We Try, We Paint" on their own during small-group or independent work time. As needed, **use the Scaffolded Support notes** that follow to guide children who need additional help.

Scaffolded Support

As needed, remind children to:

• ask questions before, during, and after they read to put into words the things they are curious about and use information from the text and pictures to try to answer their questions.

• think about why the author wrote the text.

DOK 3

Prepare to Read

GENRE STUDY ▶ **Narrative nonfiction** gives information, but it sounds like a story.

MAKE A PREDICTION ▶ Preview **We Try, We Paint**. Children go to a new room at school. What do you think they will do there?

They will paint pictures of things they like.

SET A PURPOSE ▶ Ask yourself questions before, during, and after reading to help you get information about what the children do.

28

We Try, We Paint

READ What do the children do in the new room? <u>Underline</u> it.

We see a new room at school.
We go to this room to paint.
Try to paint!
We paint the bus.
We like this bus.
This bus is great! ▶

Close Reading Tip
Put a ? by the parts you have questions about.

CHECK MY UNDERSTANDING

Write a question you have about this text.

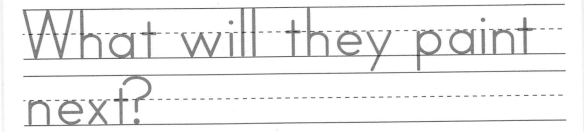

What will they paint next?

29

Scaffolded Support

As needed, remind children that:

- asking and answering questions as they read will help them understand what is happening in the text.
- they can look for clues in the words and pictures to help them figure out what the author wants them to know.

DOK 2

READ What do the children paint now? <u>Underline</u> it.

We paint the school.

We like this school.

This school is great!

We try.

We paint!

This new room is great!

We like to paint at school.

CHECK MY UNDERSTANDING

Why did the author write this text? What does the author want you to learn from it?

to give information;
Some children try to
paint and they like it.

30

DRAW IT Think about what the children paint in the room. Draw a picture of the thing you like best. Add your own details. Write a label for the picture.

Scaffolded Support

As needed, guide children to look back at the text and illustrations to recall the things the children painted. Help them label their pictures.

DOK 2

my school

31

Prepare to Read

GENRE STUDY **Realistic fiction** stories are made up but could happen in real life. Look for:

- characters who are like real people
- places that seem real
- events that could really happen

SET A PURPOSE As you read, stop and think if you don't understand something. Reread, look at the pictures, use what you already know, or ask yourself questions.

POWER WORDS

trip

partner

wished

last

Meet Elisa Chavarri.

32

My School Trip

by Aly G. Mays

illustrated by Elisa Chavarri

Monitor and Clarify

MODEL MONITORING AND CLARIFYING

💬 **THINK ALOUD** *As I read, I pause when I don't understand something. The text says they are taking a school trip. One girl doesn't look happy and excited, like the other children. I can try different things to help me understand this, like asking questions, rereading the text, looking for clues in the pictures, and thinking about what I already know.*

DOK 2

We took a school trip.

📖 **READ FOR UNDERSTANDING**

**Phonics/Decoding
in Context**

Help children point to the word *Nan*. Review that when a word has a consonant, followed by a vowel, followed by a consonant, the vowel usually stands for its short vowel sound. **Model blending** the sounds in the word: /n/ /ă/ /n/, *Nan*. Have children repeat. Point out that the name *Nan* begins and ends with the same sound.

ANNOTATION TIP: Have children underline the word *Nan*. Have them circle the letters *N* and *n*.

First, we took a bus.
Nan was my partner.

35

Notice & Note

Contrasts and Contradictions

- **Remind children** that when a character acts or feels differently from what we expect, the author is showing them something important about the character. Tell them they should stop reading to notice and note, which is a way to monitor and clarify.

- **Have children explain** why they might use this strategy on page 36. *(All the children, except for Nan, look happy to be going on a school trip.)*

ANNOTATION TIP: Have children underline the words on the page that describe feelings.

- **Remind them** of the Anchor Question: **Why might Nan feel this way?** *(Possible responses: Nan may be shy; she may be afraid.)*

DOK 2

Nan was new at school.
Was Nan mad?
Was Nan sad?

36

📖 **READ FOR UNDERSTANDING**

ASK: What happens at Butterfly Garden? (*People learn about butterflies.*)

FOLLOW-UP: What evidence lets you know? (*The illustration shows butterflies flying all around; a guide is talking to a group of children about butterflies.*)

ANNOTATION TIP: Have children circle the details in the illustrations on page 37 that help them answer the questions.

DOK 2

📖 **READ FOR UNDERSTANDING**

Quick Teach Words

As needed to support comprehension, briefly explain the meaning of *butterfly* and *garden* in this context.

- A *butterfly* is an insect that usually has beautiful wings.
- A *garden* is an area where plants, like flowers or vegetables, grow.

In this story, *Butterfly Garden* is a special place to see butterflies.

The trip was to Butterfly Garden!

37

🔍 TARGETED CLOSE READ

Author's Purpose

Have children reread pages 38–39 to start looking for clues about the author's purpose for writing.

ASK: Before you can you tell why an author wrote a text, you need to think about what the author wrote. **What kind of text this is?** (*Possible response: realistic ficton*)

FOLLOW-UP: How do you know? (*Possible response: The kids act like real kids but they aren't real.*)

DOK 3

📖 READ FOR UNDERSTANDING

Phonics/Decoding in Context

Help children point to the word *Dan*. Review that in words that have a consonant, followed by a vowel, followed by a consonant, the vowel usually stands for its short vowel sound. **Model blending** the sounds in the word: /d/ /ă/ /n/, *Dan*. Have children repeat.

Pam had a butterfly.
Dan had a butterfly.

I wished I had a butterfly.

39

I had a butterfly!
Nan was sad.

 READ FOR UNDERSTANDING

ASK: How does Nan get a butterfly?
(The girl gives her the one that was on her back.)

FOLLOW-UP: What evidence lets you know that Nan feels happy about getting a butterfly?
(The text says she's "happy at last;" the illustration shows the girl giving Nan the butterfly and Nan is smiling.)

ANNOTATION TIP: Circle the words in the text and the details in the illustrations that help you answer the questions.

DOK 2

Nan had a butterfly!
Nan was happy at last.

41

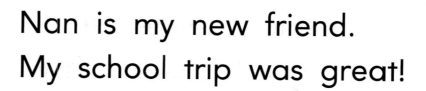

Nan is my new friend.
My school trip was great!

42

Respond to Reading

READ Together

Turn and Talk

Use details from **My School Trip** to answer these questions with a partner.

1. Monitor and Clarify When you came to a part you did not understand, what did you do to try to figure it out?

2. How can you tell that the two girls become friends?

Talking Tip

Ask a question if you are not sure about your partner's ideas.

Why did you say _____ ?

Academic Discussion

Use the TURN AND TALK routine. Remind children to follow agreed-upon rules for discussion, such as listening carefully and asking questions about things you don't understand.

Possible responses:

1. *I asked questions; I thought about what I already knew that could help me answer the questions; I reread the text; I looked for clues in the pictures.* DOK 3

2. *The picture shows the girls sitting together on the ride back to school. They are smiling. The text says that Nan is the girl's new friend.* DOK 2

43

READ
Together

Write a List

PROMPT Look back at **My School Trip**. What does the girl who is telling the story like about her trip?

PLAN First, draw or write four things the girl likes about her trip.

What the Girl Likes

WRITE Now write a list of things that the girl telling the story likes about her trip. Remember to:

- List people, places, or things the girl likes.
- Use the words and pictures from the story and your web for ideas.

Responses may vary.

Write About Reading
- **Read aloud** the Write section.
- **Encourage children** to add details from the words and pictures in the story to tell about the people, places, and things in their lists.

DOK 3

45

Independent Close Reading

Have children close read and annotate "A Trip to a Garden" on their own during small-group or independent work time. As needed, **use the Scaffolded Support notes** that follow to guide children who need additional help.

Scaffolded Support

As needed, remind children to:

• reread, look at the illustrations, ask questions, and think about what they already know to help them figure out things they do not understand.

• look for clues about the genre to help them understand the author's purpose for writing the text.

DOK 2

Prepare to Read

GENRE STUDY **Realistic fiction** stories are made up but could happen in real life.

MAKE A PREDICTION Preview **A Trip to a Garden**. A girl and her dad take a trip to a garden. What do you think they will see there?

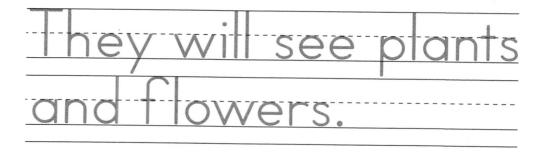

They will see plants and flowers.

SET A PURPOSE Read to find out what happens at the garden.

A Trip to a Garden

I am Nan.
This is my dad.
We like to go outside.
We go to see a garden.
This is my first trip to the garden.
We see a tan cat at the garden.
The cat likes my dad! ▶

Close Reading Tip
Put a ? by the parts you have questions about.

CHECK MY UNDERSTANDING

What do Nan and her dad see at the garden?
Go back and read again if you are not sure.

They see a tan cat.

Scaffolded Support

As needed, remind children that:

• asking and answering questions as they read will help them make sure they understand what is happening in the story.

• details in the words and pictures can help them understand more about the garden Nan and her dad visit.

DOK 2

47

READ What else do the girl and her dad see? <u>Underline</u> it. If you don't know, look at the picture for help. What else can you do to help yourself understand?

I see a butterfly at the garden.

Can my dad see the butterfly?

He can see the butterfly!

My dad is happy.

We see a new butterfly.

We like this new butterfly.

I am happy.

This is a great trip!

CHECK MY UNDERSTANDING

Why do you think the author wrote this story?

to tell a story that I would enjoy about a fun trip to a garden

48

DRAW IT Draw a picture of what Nan and her dad like about going to the garden. Write a sentence to tell about your picture.

They like the pretty butterflies.

49

READ Together

📖 **READ FOR UNDERSTANDING**

Introduce the Text

• **Read aloud** and discuss the information about the genre.

• **Guide children** to set a purpose for reading to practice how to make inferences.

• **Provide information** about the background topic, kinds of friends.

• **Tell children** to look for and think about the Power Words as they read.

Prepare to Read

GENRE STUDY **Informational text** is nonfiction. It gives facts about a topic. Look for:

• facts about friends

• headings that stand out

• photos with labels

SET A PURPOSE Read to make smart guesses, or **inferences**, about things the author does not say. Use what you already know and clues in the text and pictures to help you.

POWER WORDS
kinds
together

Build Background: Kinds of Friends

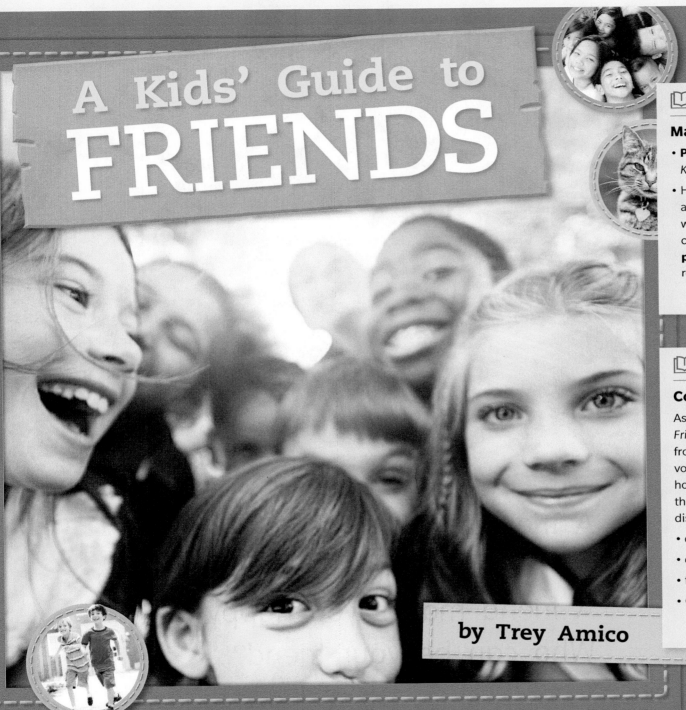

A Kids' Guide to FRIENDS

by Trey Amico

📖 READ FOR UNDERSTANDING

Make Predictions

- **Page through** the beginning of *A Kids' Guide to Friends* with children.
- Have them **use prior knowledge** and the photos and labels to predict what the text will be about. Tell children they will **return to their predictions** after they finish reading the text.

DOK 2

📖 READ FOR UNDERSTANDING

Concept Words

As children read *A Kids' Guide to Friends,* they may see familiar words from their speaking and listening vocabularies that they may not know how to read yet. Write these words on the board, read them aloud, and discuss their meanings as needed.

- cheer
- classmate
- fun
- Grandma
- hi
- sister
- sorry

Central Idea

Have children reread pages 52–53 to analyze the central idea of the text.

ASK: What is this part of the text about? (*different kinds of friends*)

FOLLOW-UP: What evidence helps you understand this? (*The text says "Kinds of Friends"; the photos show kinds of friends and the things you can do with them.*)

ANNOTATION TIP: Have children underline the details that describe what a friend is.

DOK 2

Kinds of Friends

A friend is nice.

A friend likes to be with you.

A friend makes you happy.

Who can be your friend?

52

classmate

neighbor

Grandma

Dad

sister

cat

There are all kinds of friends!

53

READ FOR UNDERSTANDING

Make Inferences
MODEL MAKING AN INFERENCE

🗨 **THINK ALOUD** *The author says there are all kinds of friends. The photos show different people and even a pet. I can use these clues to make an inference. I think the author is saying that all these people and the cat in the photos can be a friend.*

DOK 2

READ FOR UNDERSTANDING

Phonics/Decoding in Context

Help children point to the word *Dad*. Review that when a word has a consonant, followed by a vowel, followed by a consonant, the vowel usually stands for its short vowel sound. **Model blending** the sounds in the word: /d/ /ă/ /d/, *Dad*. Have children repeat. Repeat these steps with the word *cat*.

3 Big Questions

Remind children that when they are reading nonfiction, they should stop and think about the 3 Big Questions. Sometimes, they will have to make inferences to answer some of these questions.

- **What surprised me?** Tell children to pay attention to something they find interesting or something they learned.

- **What did the author think I already knew?** Have children note ideas that are confusing or words that they do not know.

- **What challenged, changed, or confirmed what I already knew?** Ask children to think about whether what they read confirmed or changed their thinking.

- **Have children** explain why they might ask themselves one or more of the 3 Big Questions on pages 54–55. (*Possible response: I can make a smart guess, or infer, that the author thought I could answer the question on this page.*)

DOK 2

Fun with Friends

Friends play.

Friends can be silly.

Friends like to be together.

What else can friends do?

54

run

dig

ride

read

jump

laugh

📖 READ FOR UNDERSTANDING

Make Inferences

ASK: Why does the author say that "the best times are with friends"?
(It's more fun to do things with friends; people are happy when they are with friends.)

FOLLOW-UP: What clues did you use to make that inference?
(Possible response: The photos show friends having a good time; I know that I always have a good time when I'm with my friends.)

ANNOTATION TIP: Have children choose the activity they most like to do with their friends from the labels and photos on this page and circle it.

DOK 2

The best times are with friends!

55

Make New Friends

School is one place to find friends.
Look around.

56

Be brave.

Say hi.

Ask someone to play with you.

57

🔍 TARGETED CLOSE READ

Central Idea

Have children reread pages 58–60 to analyze the central idea of the text.

ASK: What does the author want you to understand from reading this text? (*It's great to have friends and to be a good friend.*)

FOLLOW-UP: Which details help you figure out the central idea? (*The words say it feels good to be a friend; the photos show friends having fun together.*)

DOK 2

📖 READ FOR UNDERSTANDING

Quick Teach Words

As needed to support comprehension, briefly explain the meaning of *fair* in this context.

• If you are *fair*, you do the right thing and treat everyone the same way.

Be fair.

Take turns.

Say sorry if you make a mistake.

Cheer each other up.

What else do good friends do?

58

smile

wave

listen

share

help

play

📖 READ FOR UNDERSTANDING

Make Inferences

ASK: Why is a friend happy when you listen or help? *(Possible response: Listening and helping show that you care.)*

DOK 2

Try to make your friends happy!

59

 READ FOR UNDERSTANDING

Wrap Up

Revisit the predictions children made before reading. Have them confirm or correct their predictions using evidence from the text and pictures.

DOK 2

It feels good to be a friend.
Let's be friends!

60

Turn and Talk

Use details from **A Kids' Guide to Friends** to answer these questions with a partner.

1. **Make Inferences** Why is it a good idea to make new friends?

2. What are some different ways to be a good friend?

Talking Tip

Wait for your turn to speak. Tell about your ideas and feelings clearly.

I feel that _____.

61

Write an Opinion

PROMPT Think about the different ways to make friends in **A Kids' Guide to Friends**. Which way do you think is the best?

PLAN First, draw a picture. Show you making a new friend, using the best way you learned from **A Kids' Guide to Friends**.

Write About Reading
- **Read aloud** the prompt.
- **Lead a discussion** in which children identify the different ways to make friends that the text tells about, and which way they think is best. Tell them to use text evidence to support their ideas.
- Then read aloud the Plan section. Have children use ideas from the discussion as they create their drawings.

DOK 2

WRITE Now write a sentence to tell which way of making friends you think is the best. Then write a reason why you think it is best. Remember to:

- Tell your opinion.

- Use the word **because** when you write your reason.

Responses may vary.

Write About Reading
- **Read aloud** the Write section.
- **Prompt children** to think about their own experiences with friends to help them form an opinion. Also, encourage them to use the word *because* in their writing.

DOK 3

63

Independent Close Reading

Have children close read and annotate "Good Friends" on their own during small-group or independent work time. As needed, **use the Scaffolded Support notes** that follow to guide children who need additional help.

Scaffolded Support

As needed, remind children to:

- look for clues in the text and pictures to help them understand things the author does not say.

- use details in the text and pictures to figure out the central idea that the author wants to share.

DOK 2

Prepare to Read

GENRE STUDY **Informational text** is nonfiction. It gives facts about a topic.

MAKE A PREDICTION Preview **Good Friends**. You know that informational text has facts. What do you think you will learn from this text?

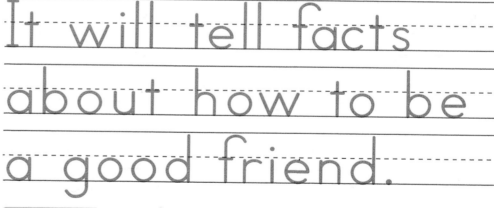

It will tell facts about how to be a good friend.

SET A PURPOSE Read to find out some of the things good friends do.

64

Good Friends

READ Think about what the text is mainly about.

Good friends like to go to school together.
Friends like to go outside.
A friend is sad.
A good friend is sorry.
A friend is mad.
A good friend is fair. ▶

Close Reading Tip

Mark important ideas with *.

CHECK MY UNDERSTANDING

How can you help a friend who is sad or mad?

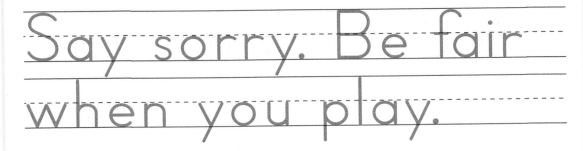

Say sorry. Be fair
when you play.

65

READ How can you help a new classmate? <u>Underline</u> it.

A classmate is new at school.

At first, the classmate is sad.

A good friend is brave.

Go to the new classmate.

This is a new friend.

The new friend is happy!

New friends enjoy school together.

CHECK MY UNDERSTANDING

What is the main thing, or central idea, the text is about?

There are many different ways to be a good friend.

66

Cite Text Evidence

WRITE ABOUT IT Think about how the good friends act in **Good Friends**. Why do you think the new friend is happy?

The new friend is happy because now he has someone to play with and talk to.

67

Scaffolded Support

As needed, guide children to think about the words and the pictures to make a good guess about why the boy feels happy.

DOK 2

Prepare to Read

GENRE STUDY **Fairy tales** are old stories that have made-up characters and events that could not happen. Look for:

- phrases like **Once upon a time**
- a happy ending

SET A PURPOSE **Ask questions** before, during, and after you read to help you understand the text and get information. Look for evidence in the text and pictures to **answer** your questions.

POWER WORDS

ugly

paddled

chilly

beautiful

changed

Meet Gail Carson Levine.

Big Dilly's Tale

by Gail Carson Levine
illustrated by Jui Ishida

Ask and Answer Questions

MODEL ASKING AND ANSWERING A QUESTION

💬 **THINK ALOUD** *Before, during, and after I read, I ask myself questions about the story. As I read, I ask myself questions about things I don't understand. I read that a duck called Dilly ugly. I ask myself, why does the duck think Dilly is ugly? I look at the picture to see if that helps answer my question. It does! I think the duck says Dilly is ugly just because Dilly looks different from the other ducks.*

DOK 2

🔍 **TARGETED CLOSE READ**

Characters

Have children reread pages 70–71 to identify the story characters.

ASK: Who are the characters in the story? *(two friends, Dilly and Minna)*

FOLLOW-UP: What do you know about them? *(Dilly looks different from Minna and the other ducks; Dilly and Minna like to have fun together.)*

ANNOTATION TIP: Have children underline the words that describe Dilly.

DOK 2

70

Once upon a time, Dilly was a BIG duckling with a BIG beak. A duck called him ugly.

 READ FOR UNDERSTANDING

**Phonics/Decoding
in Context**

Help children point to the word *His*. Review that when a word has a consonant, followed by a vowel, followed by a consonant, the vowel usually stands for its short vowel sound. **Model blending** the sounds in the word: /h/ /ĭ/ /z/, *His*. Have children repeat. Then repeat the steps with the word *him*.

His friend Minna called him cute.
Dilly splashed. Splat!

71

One day, Dilly paddled fast for fun.

But when he turned, he was alone.

And lost.

And afraid.

READ FOR UNDERSTANDING

ASK: Why is Dilly alone? (*Possible responses: Minna could not swim as fast as Dilly; Dilly was having so much fun, he didn't think about where he was going.*)

ANNOTATION TIP: Have children underline the words that tell how Dilly feels.

FOLLOW-UP: What do you think Dilly will do? (*Accept reasonable responses.*)

DOK 2

The next morning, a chilly wind blew.
Dilly wished for Minna.

73

Quick Teach Words

As needed to support comprehension, briefly explain the meaning of *farm* in this context

- A *farm* is a piece of land where crops grow and animals live.

Then Dilly saw a girl.
She led him to her farm.

74

The barn was warm.

Dilly found a nest just his size!

He lived at the farm for many weeks.

 TARGETED CLOSE READ

Characters

Have children reread pages 76–77 to analyze the characters.

ASK: Why do you think Dilly went to find Minna? *(Possible response: because she is his friend)*

FOLLOW-UP: How do you know? *(The words say that Minna thinks Dilly is cute; The pictures show that Dilly and Minna like spending time together.)*

DOK 2

📖 **READ FOR UNDERSTANDING**

Quick Teach Words

As needed to support comprehension, briefly explain the meaning of *spring* in this context.

• *Spring* is the season after winter and before summer. It is the time of year when plants begin to grow.

When spring came,
Dilly went to find Minna.
He saw the ducks!
And he saw swans.

76

Dilly looked at himself.

Oh! He saw a swan!

Dilly was not a duck after all!

Minna said he was still cute.

77

Ask and Answer Questions

MODEL ASKING AND ANSWERING A QUESTION

💬 **THINK ALOUD** *After reading a story, I ask questions to be sure I understand what I read. I ask, What was the story mostly about? What did the character learn? If I'm not sure how to answer my questions, I look back at the text and pictures to help me answer them.*

ASK: What questions do you have about this story? How will you answer your questions? *(Accept reasonable responses.)*

DOK 2

Wrap Up

Revisit the predictions children made before reading. Have them confirm or correct their predictions using evidence from the text and pictures.

DOK 2

Honk! Ha!

Quack! Ha!

Dilly played with the swans and Minna and the other ducks. He lived happily ever after!

78

Use details from **Big Dilly's Tale** to answer these questions with a partner.

1. **Ask and Answer Questions** What questions did you ask yourself about Dilly before, during, and after reading? How did they help you understand the story?

2. What does Dilly learn about himself?

Talking Tip

Complete the sentence to add to what your partner says.

My idea is _____.

79

Write a Description

PROMPT What is Dilly like in **Big Dilly's Tale**? Use ideas from the words and pictures in the story to help you describe Dilly.

PLAN First, write words to tell what Dilly looks like. Tell how he sounds and acts.

Looks	Sounds	Acts

WRITE Now write sentences to describe what Dilly is like and why he does the things he does. Remember to:

Big Dilly's Tale

- Use words that tell how Dilly looks, sounds, and acts. Tell why he acts that way.

- Put a period at the end of each sentence.

Responses may vary.

Write About Reading
- **Read aloud** the Write section.
- **Encourage children** to add details to their sentences that tell more about what Dilly is like. In addition, prompt them to add a period at the end of their sentences.

DOK 3

Prepare to Read

GENRE STUDY **Fairy tales** are old stories that have made-up characters and events that could not happen.

MAKE A PREDICTION Preview **The Map**. A brave duck wants to find new friends. Where do you think the duck will look for them?

The duck will look
on a farm.

SET A PURPOSE Ask yourself questions about **The Map** before, during, and after reading to help you find out what Duck does and to understand the story.

82

The Map

READ How does Duck get to the farm? <u>Underline</u> words that tell.

Brave Duck took a trip to find new friends.
She had a map.
Tap, tap, tap, on the map!
The map took Duck to a farm.
Sad Cat was at the farm.
Sad Cat was happy to see Duck.
Duck had a new friend! ▶

Close Reading Tip

Put a ? by the parts you have questions about.

Scaffolded Support

As needed, guide children to:

- reread the text to look for details that will help them answer the question.

- use what they know about the characters to predict where they might go next.

- ask and answer questions about the text.

DOK 2

CHECK MY UNDERSTANDING

Write a question you have about the story.

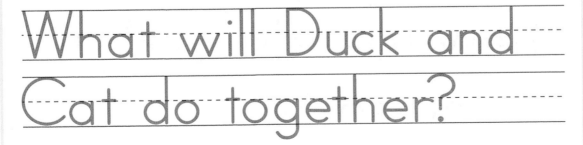

What will Duck and Cat do together?

83

READ Duck and Cat use the amazing map. Where do they go? Who do they meet? <u>Underline</u> words that tell.

Close Reading Tip

Write C when you make a connection.

Duck and Cat wished to find a new friend.
Tap, tap, tap, on the map!
The map took Duck and Cat to a garden.
Sad Butterfly was in the garden.
Sad Butterfly was happy to see Duck and Cat.
Duck had new friends at last!
Then the new friends had fun together.

Scaffolded Support

As needed, remind children that:

- when they make connections, they find ways that the story is like and unlike things in other parts of the story or in the real world.
- they can ask themselves questions about how the characters feel and how their feelings change during the story.

DOK 2

CHECK MY UNDERSTANDING

How does Duck feel at the end of the story? Why?

Duck is happy. She took a trip to find new friends, and she found some.

WRITE ABOUT IT What do Duck, Cat, and Butterfly do now? Add to the story. Draw a picture on another sheet of paper to go with your writing.

Responses will vary but should add on to the story.

85

VIEW FOR UNDERSTANDING

Introduce the Video

- **Read aloud** and discuss the information about the genre.
- Guide children to **set a purpose** for viewing to learn about the characters.
- Provide information about brothers John and Jacob—the creators of the FuZees.

Prepare to View

 **Songs** are words set to music. We can sing them out loud. Listen for:

- the tune, or how the song sounds
- words that repeat
- how the song makes you feel

 Watch to find out who the **characters** are and what they look like. Find out what the characters do and say. This will help you understand how they feel and why they act the way they do.

Meet The FuZees.

86

I'M ME

by The FuZees

📖 **VIEW FOR UNDERSTANDING**

Make Predictions
- **Display** the cover of *I'm Me* for children.
- Have them **use prior knowledge** and the opening picture to predict what the video will be about. Tell children they will **return to their predictions** after they finish watching the video.

DOK 2

As You View Get to know the characters! Think about the words of the song. Watch for the pictures that pop up. Use details in the pictures and the song to help you understand what the characters like, what makes them special, and why they act the way they do.

 VIEW FOR UNDERSTANDING

Characters

ASK: Who are the characters in the video? *(two brothers, Jacob and Josh)*

FOLLOW-UP: What makes each character special? *(Possible responses: The characters like different things and they like to do different things.)*

DOK 2

88

I'M ME
by The FaZoos

Use details from **I'm Me** to answer these questions with a partner.

1. **Characters** Describe what the characters are like. What things do they like? Why do the characters do the things they do?

2. Why do the characters think it is good to be unique?

Listening Tip

Listen carefully and politely. Look at your partner to show that you are paying attention.

Academic Discussion

Use the TURN AND TALK routine.
Remind children to follow agreed-upon rules for discussion, such as listening carefully and looking at their partner to show they are listening.

Possible responses:

1. *Each brother likes different things, like different colors, music, and clothing; they do those things because it makes them feel happy.* DOK 1

2. *They think it's good to be unique because the things that make you different are the things that make you be you!* DOK 2

89

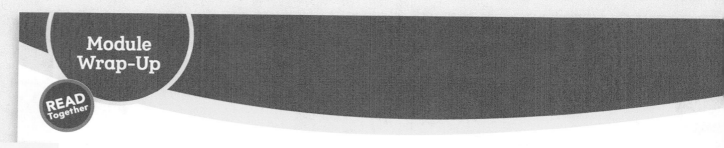

**Revisit the
Essential Question**

• **Read aloud** the Essential Question.

• **Remind children** that in this
module, they read different texts
about the topic of new friends and
experiences that can help them
answer the question.

• **Have children** choose one of the
activities to show what they learned
in this module.

Welcome to Our Class!

• **Encourage children** to revisit the
stories and think about what it
means to be a good friend. Many of
these ideas can also help a new
student feel welcome. For example,
sharing, listening, playing, and
helping would help a new student
feel welcome in the classroom.

• **Guide children** to share their posters
in a small group. Have them read the
labels and phrases on their posters.

DOK 3

Let's Wrap Up!

(?) Essential Question

How can making new friends and learning new things help us?

Pick one of these activities to show what
you have learned about the topic.

1. Welcome to Our Class!

How could you help a new
student feel welcome in
your class? Make a
poster with words and
pictures. Use ideas from
the texts you have read
about friends.

90

2. Cheer for Friends!

Think about something new you and a friend tried to do or want to try to do. Make up a cheer that describes it. Practice the cheer. Then share it with the class.

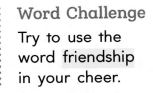

Word Challenge

Try to use the word friendship in your cheer.

Cheer for Friends!

- **Explain that** most cheers have rhyming words. After children choose a topic for the cheer, guide them to list pairs of rhyming words that they can use in their cheer. Encourage them to use the word *friendship* in the cheer.

- **Have children** practice the cheer several times, focusing on the rhythm of the words. Help them make word changes to improve the rhythm.

DOK 3

Brainstorm and Plan

Have children use the My Notes space to jot down ideas for their chosen activity. Remind them to refer back to their notes as they complete the activity.

My Notes

91

Introduce the Topic

- **Read aloud** the module title, *My Family, My Community.*
- **Tell children** that in this module they will be reading texts about communities.
- **Have children** share prior knowledge about the topic or word associations for communities. Record their ideas in a web.

Discuss the Quotation

- **Read aloud** the Hispanic proverb.
- **Lead a discussion** in which children try to explain the quote in their own words. Explain the meaning, as needed: *Your home is where your loved ones are.*

ASK: What does home mean to you? *(Accept reasonable responses.)*

MODULE 2

My Family, My Community

"Your heart will lead you home!"

—Hispanic Proverb

92

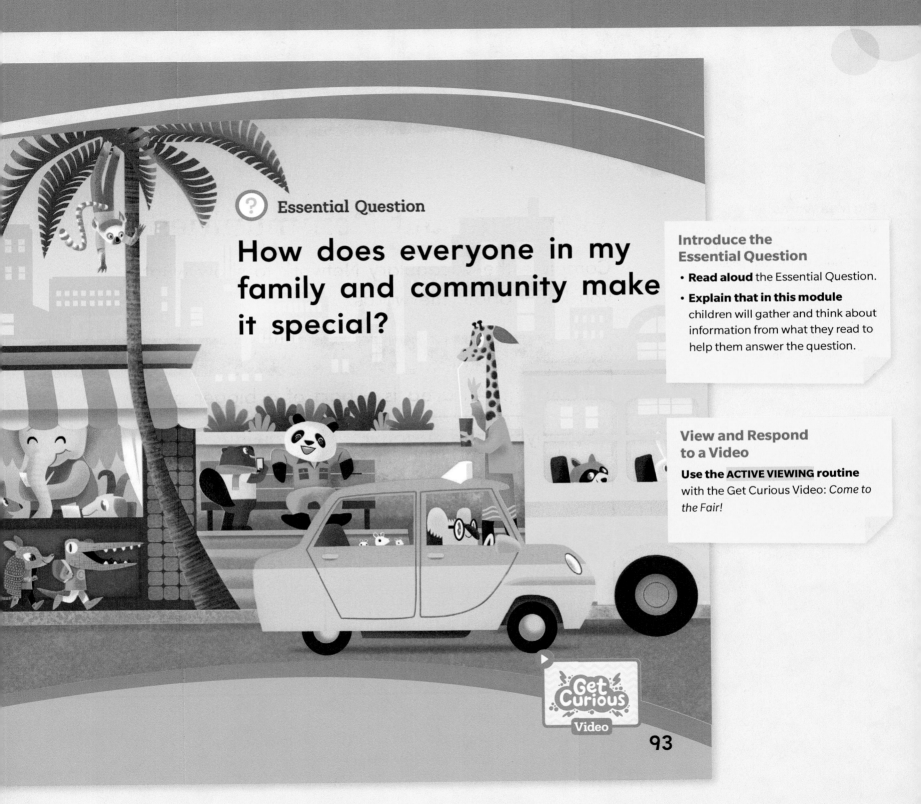

How does everyone in my family and community make it special?

Introduce the Essential Question

- **Read aloud** the Essential Question.
- **Explain that in this module** children will gather and think about information from what they read to help them answer the question.

View and Respond to a Video

Use the ACTIVE VIEWING routine with the Get Curious Video: *Come to the Fair!*

Get Curious Video

93

Big Idea Words

Use the VOCABULARY routine and the Vocabulary Cards to introduce the Big Idea Words *area, population,* and *working.* You may wish to display the corresponding Vocabulary Card for each word as you discuss it.

1. Say the Big Idea Word.

2. Explain the meaning.

3. Talk about examples.

Vocabulary Network

• **Prompt children** to think about places they go that are part of a bigger *area.*

Words About Communities

Complete the Vocabulary Network to show what you know about the words.

area

Meaning: An **area** is a part of a bigger place.

Synonyms and Antonyms	Drawing

population

Meaning: The **population** is the number of people who live in a place.

Synonyms and Antonyms	Drawing

working

Meaning: If you are **working**, you are doing a job.

Synonyms and Antonyms	Drawing

Vocabulary Network

- **Point out** to children that a *population* can be any size. They may want to draw just a few people or fill the drawing space with many people.

- **As children complete** the activity for *working*, prompt them to think of jobs they know about and how people do those jobs.

95

Kids Speak Up!

Why is the place where you live great?

I think my town is great!
It has a big park.
We can play ball.

I like my town
because it has
a library. I get
tons of books!

The workers make my town great. Firefighters put out fires FAST!

I love my town!
It has a lake.
My dad and
I go fishing.

📖 READ FOR UNDERSTANDING

Ideas and Support

ASK: What are all of these kids trying to persuade you to think? *(They want you to think that their town is great.)*

FOLLOW-UP: How do they try to persuade you? *(They each give a reason why they think their town is great.)*

ANNOTATION TIP: Ask children to underline the words that tell each child's reason for thinking his or her town is great.

DOK 3

97

READ
Together

 READ FOR UNDERSTANDING

Introduce the Text

• **Read aloud** and discuss the information about the genre.

• **Guide children** to set a purpose for reading to practice retelling the important parts of the story.

• **Provide information** about the author and illustrator, Wong Herbert Yee.

• **Tell children** to look for and think about the Power Words as they read.

Prepare to Read

GENRE STUDY **Realistic fiction** stories are made up but could happen in real life. Look for:

• characters who have problems that real people might have

• places that seem real

SET A PURPOSE Read to understand events in the beginning, middle, and end. Look for details in the words and pictures to help you. **Retell** the events in your own words.

POWER WORDS
mess
market
sell
help
neighbors
set

Meet Wong Herbert Yee.

98

Dan Had a Plan

by Wong Herbert Yee

📖 READ FOR UNDERSTANDING

Make Predictions

- **Page through** the beginning of *Dan Had a Plan* with children.
- Have them **use prior knowledge** and the illustrations to predict what the story will be about. Tell children they will **return to their predictions** after they finish reading the story.

DOK 2

📖 READ FOR UNDERSTANDING

Concept Words

As children read *Dan Had a Plan*, they may see familiar words from their speaking and listening vocabularies that they may not know how to read yet. Write these words on the board, read them aloud, and discuss their meanings as needed.

- asked
- books
- bugs
- farmers'
- library
- money
- sign

"Hi, Dan," said Kim.
"Can you see my bugs and bats?"
"I see a big mess!" said Dan.

100

READ FOR UNDERSTANDING

Retell

MODEL RETELLING

🔍 **THINK ALOUD** *Retelling a story can help me understand it. When I retell a story, I use my own words to tell what happens. At the beginning of this story, Kim is in their kitchen making fruit snacks to sell at a farmers' market. The family is going to sell them to make money for new library books.*

DOK 2

"We will go to the farmers' market.
We will sell the bugs and bats.
The money is for new library books."

101

Setting

Have children reread pages 102–103 to identify and describe the setting.

ASK: What is the setting in this part of the story? *(the family's home and then the farmers' market)*

FOLLOW-UP: What evidence tells you this? *(The pictures show the family at their house and then outside, where people are selling things.)*

DOK 2

📖 READ FOR UNDERSTANDING

Phonics/Decoding in Context

Have children point to the word *Kim*. Remind them that they can use what they know about consonant sounds to help them read words. Review that the consonant *k* stands for the /k/ sound. **Model blending** the sounds in the word: /k/ /ĭ/ /m/, *Kim*. Have children repeat. Point out that *Kim* is a name and that names begin with a capital letter.

ANNOTATION TIP: Have children add the words *Kim* and *Dan* as labels on the picture.

"I like bugs and bats," said Dan.
"I like books. Can I help?"
"You are too little," said Kim.

102

📖 **READ FOR UNDERSTANDING**

ASK: What does the author mean when he says that Dad and the neighbors "set up"? *(Dad and the neighbors get ready to sell their things, like putting a tablecloth on a table and putting up an umbrella.)*

FOLLOW-UP: What evidence lets you know? *(The picture shows Dad standing at a table, ready to sell the snacks. There are other tables around him with different things to sell.)*

DOK 2

Dad and the neighbors set up.
"Hi, kids!" said Dad.

103

Aha Moment

- **Remind children** that when they are reading and a character realizes something, they should stop to notice and note because it means that something in the story will likely change. Explain that retelling what has happened so far can help them think about how the story might change.

- **Have children** tell how this strategy can help them on page 105. *(When Dan sees the sign on their table, he gets an idea about how he can help.)*

ANNOTATION TIP: Have children circle the detail in the picture that gives Dan the idea for his plan.

- **Remind children** of the Anchor Question: **How might this change things?** *(Dan's plan might help the family sell more snacks.)*

DOK 3

📖 **READ FOR UNDERSTANDING**

Quick Teach Words As needed to support comprehension, briefly explain the meaning of *plan* in this context.

- When you have a *plan*, you have an idea about how to do something.

DOK 1

"Did you see the big sign?" asked Dan.
Dan had a plan.
"We can help!" said Dan.

105

READING FOR UNDERSTANDING

Retell

MODEL RETELLING

💬 THINK ALOUD *I will pause here to check that I understand what is happening. I can use the words and pictures to help me retell this part of the story: When Dan and his family get to the market, Dan thinks of a way that he and his friend can help. He takes the sign from their table and walks around with his friend Sam. They tell people they can help the library by buying their fruit snacks.*

DOK 2

READ FOR UNDERSTANDING

ASK: Why does the author show Dan and Sam's words in capital letters? *(to show that Dan and Sam are yelling or using very loud voices)*

DOK 2

Help the Library!

"BUY A BUG!" said Dan.
"BUY A BAT!" said Sam.

READ FOR UNDERSTANDING

ASK: How does Sam help Dan?
(He tells their friends how good the snacks are.)

ANNOTATION TIP: Have children underline the word that Sam says in a loud voice.

DOK 2

"Is it good?" asked Tim.

"It is GREAT!" said Sam.

Tim ran to buy a bat.

107

"Can I buy a bug?" asked Pam.
"You can!" said Dan.

Many neighbors had bugs and bats.

READ FOR UNDERSTANDING

Retell

ASK: What is happening in this part of the story? Tell about it in your own words. *(Dan and Sam tell people about the bugs and bats. Lots of people buy the bugs and bats.)*

DOK 2

109

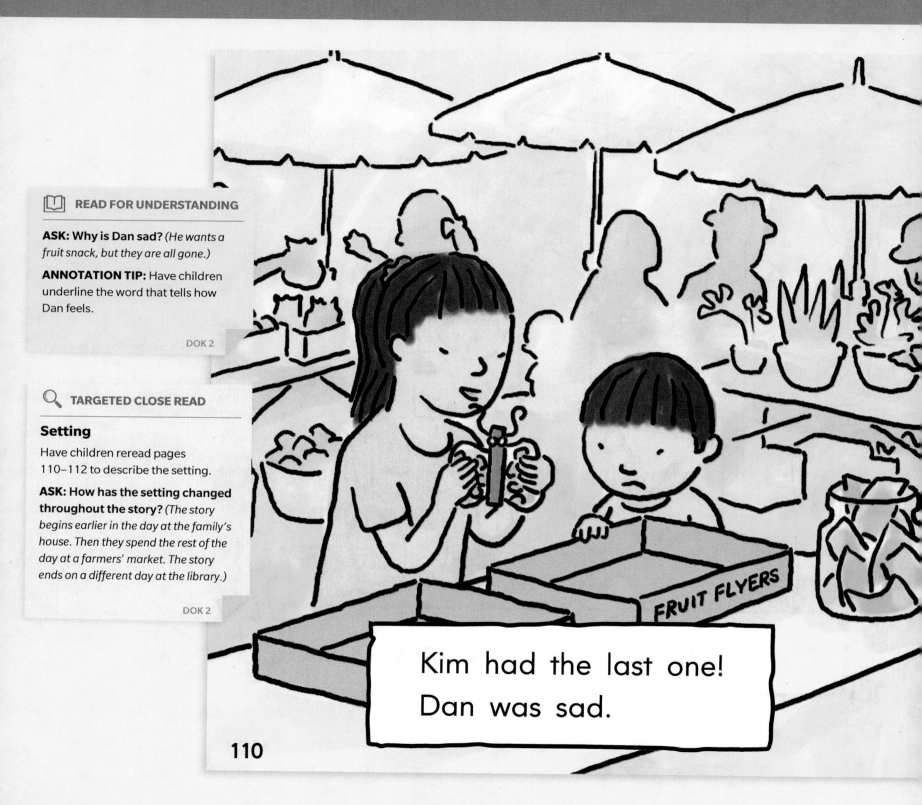

READ FOR UNDERSTANDING

ASK: Why is Dan sad? *(He wants a fruit snack, but they are all gone.)*

ANNOTATION TIP: Have children underline the word that tells how Dan feels.

DOK 2

TARGETED CLOSE READ

Setting

Have children reread pages 110–112 to describe the setting.

ASK: How has the setting changed throughout the story? *(The story begins earlier in the day at the family's house. Then they spend the rest of the day at a farmers' market. The story ends on a different day at the library.)*

DOK 2

FRUIT FLYERS

Kim had the last one!
Dan was sad.

110

"You are little," said Kim.
"You are a big help, too!"

New Books

The new books are at the library. "We did it!" said Dan and Sam.

112

Use details from **Dan Had a Plan** to answer these questions with a partner.

1. **Retell** Tell the story in your own words. Tell the main things that happen first, next, and last.

2. How does Kim feel about Dan at the end of the story? Why?

Listening Tip

Look at your partner. Show that you are interested in what your partner says.

113

Cite Text Evidence

READ Together

Write a Plan

PROMPT Look back at **Dan Had a Plan**. What steps do Dan and Sam follow to sell the fruit snacks?

PLAN First, write or draw what Dan and Sam do first, next, and last in their plan.

First

Next

Last

114

Write About Reading

- **Read aloud** the prompt.
- **Lead a discussion** in which children identify the steps that Dan and Sam take to sell the fruit snacks. Tell them to use text evidence to support their ideas.
- Then read aloud the Plan section. Have children use ideas from the discussion in their drawings or writings.

DOK 3

WRITE Now write sentences to explain what Dan and Sam do to sell the fruit snacks. Remember to:

- Use the words **first**, **next**, and **last**.

- Begin each sentence with a capital letter. End it with a period.

Responses may vary.

Write About Reading
- **Read aloud** the Write section.
- **Encourage children** to use their flow charts to help them explain the events in order, using the words *first*, *next*, and *last*. Have children begin each sentence with a capital letter and end it with a period.

DOK 2

115

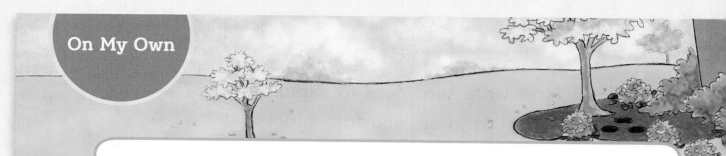

Prepare to Read

GENRE STUDY **Realistic fiction** stories are made up but could happen in real life.

MAKE A PREDICTION Preview **Together**. Three friends like to help their neighbors. What do you think they will do?

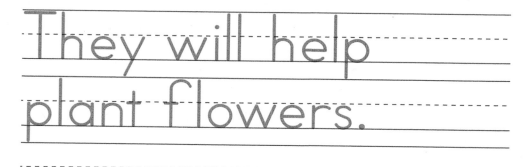

They will help plant flowers.

SET A PURPOSE Read to find out how the friends help their neighbors. Find out if your prediction is right.

116

Together

READ How do the kids help? <u>Underline</u> words that tell.

Kim, Pam, and Sam are friends.
The kids like this neighborhood.
The kids like to help the neighbors.
A neighbor asked, "Can you help dig?"
"We will help you dig!"
Kim, Pam, and Sam did it together. ▶

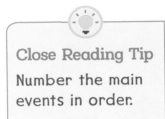

Close Reading Tip
Number the main events in order.

CHECK MY UNDERSTANDING

Describe the setting of the story.

a neighborhood yard
on a fall day

Scaffolded Support

As needed, guide children to:

• look for words that tell about the kids' actions.

• use details in the text and pictures to identify where and when the story takes place.

• think about the order in which the events happen.

DOK 2

117

Close Reading Tip

Put a ! by a
surprising part.

READ How do the kids help more neighbors?

A neighbor asked, "Can you see this big mess?"

"We will help you!" said the kids.

A neighbor asked "Can you find my cat?"

"We will help you find the cat."

Then the neighbors asked, "Can you sip this?"

And the kids had many sips—happy together!

Scaffolded Support

As needed, remind children that:

• they can use clues from the text and picture to help them answer the question.

• an author may include unexpected events in a story to make the reading more enjoyable.

DOK 2

CHECK MY UNDERSTANDING

How does the story end? How do the kids feel?

The neighbors give
the kids lemonade.
They are happy.

118

DRAW IT Draw pictures of the ways the kids help their neighbors. Then tell the story to a partner in your own words. Use your pictures to help you. Tell the main events that happen first, next, and last.

Pictures should show the kids digging, raking leaves, and finding a cat.

Scaffolded Support

As needed, guide children to number their drawings and use the words *first, next,* and *last* as they retell the story.

DOK 2

READ
Together

READ FOR UNDERSTANDING

Introduce the Text

- **Read aloud** and discuss the information about the genre.
- **Guide children** to set a purpose for reading to practice summarizing important ideas.
- **Provide information** about the background topic, Where We Live.
- **Tell children** to look for and think about the Power Words as they read.

Prepare to Read

GENRE STUDY **Informational text** is nonfiction. It gives facts about a topic. Look for:

- photographs
- maps that help explain a topic
- details and facts about a topic

SET A PURPOSE Read to understand what the most important ideas are. Look for details in the words and pictures to help you. **Summarize** by telling the important ideas in your own words.

POWER WORDS
town
map

Build Background: Where We Live

120

On the Map!

by Lisa Fleming

📖 **READ FOR UNDERSTANDING**

Make Predictions

- **Page through** the beginning of *On the Map!* with children.

- Have them **use prior knowledge** and the photographs and maps to predict what the text will be about. Tell children they will **return to their predictions** after they finish reading the text.

DOK 2

📖 **READ FOR UNDERSTANDING**

Concept Words

As children read *On the Map!* they may see familiar words from their speaking and listening vocabularies that they may not know how to read yet. Write these words on the board, read them aloud, and discuss their meanings as needed.

- city
- neighborhoods
- suburb

This is a town.
What do you see in the town?

Key

🏠 house
🏬 store
🏫 school
🏛 library
〰 bridge
⬎ street
〜 river

This is a map of a town.
What do you see on the map?

123

Summarize

MODEL SUMMARIZING

💬 **THINK ALOUD** *When I read, I want to be sure I understand the most important ideas. I ask myself: What have I learned so far? What are the most important details? I can summarize what I read so far to be sure I understand it: A town is a place that has many different kinds of buildings. A map of a town shows where the buildings, streets, and other things in the town are located.*

DOK 2

🔍 **TARGETED CLOSE READ**

Text Features

Have children reread page 123 to analyze text features.

ASK: What do the map and the symbols show? *(The map shows where different places are in a town and the symbols tell what each place is.)*

FOLLOW-UP: Why do you think the author included a map and symbols? *(Possible response: To show, instead of tell, what a town looks like.)*

ANNOTATION TIP: *Have children draw a line from each of the symbols in the Key to a place on the map.*

DOK 2

This is a big city.
What do you see in the city?

124

Key

- 🏢 office
- 🏬 store
- 🏫 school
- 🏦 bank
- 🏥 hospital
- 🍽 restaurant
- 🏠 house
- 🛣 street
- 🌳 park

N W E S

This is a map of a big city.
What do you see on the map?

125

📖 **READ FOR UNDERSTANDING**

Summarize

ASK: What do you learn on pages 124–125? Use your own words to summarize. *(A big city has lots of tall buildings that are close together. A map of the city shows what the different kinds of buildings are and where they are located.)*

DOK 3

📖 **READ FOR UNDERSTANDING**

READ FOR UNDERSTANDING
ASK: Which places do you see in the big city that you do not see in the town? *(office, bank, hospital, restaurant, and park)*

FOLLOW-UP: How do you know? *(I compared the two map keys.)*

ANNOTATION TIP: Have children circle the names of the places in the Key that they see in the big city but they do not see in the town.

DOK 3

Text Features

Have children reread page 126 to analyze text features.

ASK: Why does the author include the photos and labels on this page? *(to show two places where people live)*

FOLLOW-UP: How do the labels help you? *(The labels name the places shown in the photos.)*

ANNOTATION TIP: Have children circle the labels on the page.

DOK 3

READ FOR UNDERSTANDING

Wrap Up

Revisit the predictions children made before reading. Have them confirm or correct their predictions using evidence from the text and pictures.

DOK 2

suburb

farm

My Neighborhood

We live in many kinds of neighborhoods.
What is your map like?

126

Turn and Talk

Use details from **On the Map!** to answer these questions with a partner.

1. **Summarize** What are the most important facts you learned?

2. How is a town like a city? How is it different?

Talking Tip

Ask a question if you are not sure about your partner's ideas.

Why did you say _____?

Academic Discussion

Use the TURN AND TALK routine. Remind children to use complete sentences when they share their ideas and to ask questions about things they do not understand.

Possible responses:

1. *A map is a picture of a real place that shows buildings, streets, and other things in it. A map can show different kinds of places, such as towns and big cities.* DOK 2

2. *A town is like a city because they both have the same kinds of buildings and streets. A town is different than a city because it is smaller in size, it has smaller buildings, and there is more land around the buildings.* DOK 3

127

Cite Text Evidence

READ Together

Write Directions

PROMPT Choose a map from **On the Map!** How do you get from one place to another?

PLAN First, draw or write where you start and then how to get from that place to the other place. Do you turn? What do you pass?

First

↓

Next

↓

Last

128

Write About Reading

- **Read aloud** the prompt.
- **Lead a discussion** in which children use location words to tell how they can get from one place on the map to another. Tell them to use text evidence to support their ideas.
- Then read aloud the Plan section. Have children use ideas from the discussion in their drawings or writings.

DOK 2

WRITE Now write directions that tell how to get from one place to another. Remember to:

- Tell each step in order.
- Use the words **first**, **next**, and **last**. Spell them correctly.

Responses may vary.

Write About Reading

- **Read aloud** the Write section.
- **Encourage children** to refer to the map as they write each step of their directions in order, using the words *first*, *next*, and *last*.

DOK 2

129

On My Own

farm

N W E S

Independent Close Reading

Have children close read and annotate "Neighborhoods" on their own during small-group or independent work time. As needed, **use the Scaffolded Support notes** that follow to guide children who need additional help.

Scaffolded Support

As needed, remind children to:

• use their own words to summarize the most important ideas in the text.

• look for special features, such as bold text, labels, maps, and symbols to help them understand and locate information.

DOK 2

Prepare to Read

GENRE STUDY **Informational text** is nonfiction. It gives facts about a topic.

MAKE A PREDICTION Preview **Neighborhoods**. Look at the text features, like the map, labels, symbols, and bold text. What do you think you will learn?

I will learn about city and farm neighborhoods.

SET A PURPOSE Read to find out about neighborhoods in different places.

130

city

Neighborhoods

Key
— street
🏠 house
🏢 office
🏫 school

READ <u>Underline</u> words the author wants you to notice.

What is a **city** like?
A city is big!
It has many **neighborhoods**.
You can see many neighbors.
You can go on a bus to a school,
a library, and a market. ▶

Close Reading Tip
Mark important
ideas with *.

CHECK MY UNDERSTANDING

What important ideas did you learn from the map and text?

A city is big; has lots
of people and places.

131

READ What is this part mostly about?

What is a **farm** like?
A farm is not as big as a city.
It is outside the city.
You do not see many neighbors.
You can go on a bus to school,
just like in a city.
Is your neighborhood like a farm?
Is it like a city?

Close Reading Tip

Circle words you don't know. Then figure them out.

Scaffolded Support

As needed, guide children to:

• think about what they learned from this section and tell the important ideas in their own words.

• determine word meaning by rereading the sentence for context clues, asking for help, or using a dictionary.

DOK 2

CHECK MY UNDERSTANDING

How is the city different from the farm neighborhood?

A city is bigger. It has more people and buildings.

WRITE ABOUT IT What would it be like to live in a city or on a farm? Choose one to write about. Tell what the place is like. Use ideas from the text and pictures in **Neighborhoods**.

I would like to live in a city. It has lots of neighbors. I would have lots of friends. I would ride a bus to school and to go see many places.

Scaffolded Support

As needed, guide children to use what they already know and what they learned in the text to describe what it would be like to live in a city or a farm.

DOK 2

133

READ FOR UNDERSTANDING

Introduce the Text

- **Read aloud** and discuss the information about the genre.
- **Guide children** to set a purpose for reading to make connections to their own lives and other texts.
- **Provide information** about the background topic, City Neighborhoods.
- **Tell children** to look for and think about the Power Words as they read.

Prepare to Read

GENRE STUDY **Informational text** is nonfiction. It gives facts about a topic. Look for:

- facts about the world
- photos of real people and places
- headings that tell what each part is about

SET A PURPOSE As you read, **make connections** by finding ways that this text is like things in your life and other texts you have read. This will help you understand and remember the text.

POWER WORDS

community

places

purpose

clinic

Build Background: City Neighborhoods

134

Places in My Neighborhood

by Shelly Lyons

📖 READ FOR UNDERSTANDING

Make Predictions

- **Page through** the beginning of *Places in My Neighborhood* with children.

- Have them **use prior knowledge** and the photographs and headings to predict what the text will be about. Tell children they will **return to their predictions** after they finish reading the text.

DOK 2

📖 READ FOR UNDERSTANDING

Concept Words

As children read *Places in My Neighborhood*, they may see familiar words from their speaking and listening vocabularies that they may not know how to read yet. Write these words on the board, read them aloud, and discuss their meanings as needed.

- firefighters
- police
- nurse
- safe
- officer
- station

What Is a Neighborhood?

A neighborhood is a community filled with different places to see. Each place has a special purpose that meets our needs.

136

Places to Live

Mia's home is in the city.

Her apartment is in a building

with many other apartments.

Make Connections
MODEL MAKING A CONNECTION

💬 **THINK ALOUD** *This reminds me of the text we read called On the Map! That text was also about different places where people live and work, except that On the Map! had a photo and a map of the city. This text only has photos.*

DOK 3

🔍 **TARGETED CLOSE READ**

Content-Area Words
Have children reread pages 137–138 to analyze the meaning of the words *city* and *town*.

ASK: How can the heading help you figure out the meaning of city?
(It says the page is about places to live, so a city must be a place where people live.)

FOLLOW-UP: How can the photo help you know what city means?
(The photo shows many houses and apartments, so a city must be a place where a lot of people live.)

ANNOTATION TIP: Have children circle the heading and underline the word *city*.

DOK 2

137

Jack lives in a house

in a small town.

His street is lined with homes.

138

Places to Keep Us Safe

Carlos visits the fire station
in his neighborhood.
The firefighters rush
to put out a fire.

Notice & Note

3 Big Questions

- **Remind children** that when they are reading an informational text, they should stop and think about the 3 Big Questions. Sometimes they will have to make connections to answer some of these questions.
- **What surprised me?** Tell children to pay attention to something they find interesting or something they learned from the text.
- **What did the author think I already knew?** Have children note ideas that are confusing or words they do not know.
- **What challenged, changed, or confirmed what I already knew?** Ask children to think about whether what they read confirmed or changed their thinking.
- Have children explain why they might ask themselves one or more of the 3 Big Questions on page 139. (*I might ask myself one of these questions to help me make a connection to what I already know about how firefighters keep us safe.*)

DOK 3

Devon visits the police station.

The officer tells him

not to talk to strangers.

140

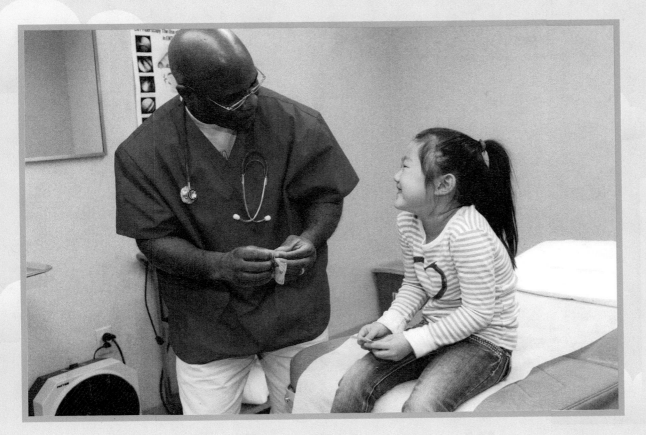

📖 **READ FOR UNDERSTANDING**

Make Connections

ASK: How do people at a clinic help others? (*They take care of them when they are sick or get hurt.*)

FOLLOW-UP: When have you been to a clinic? Who took care of you? What did that person do? (*Responses will vary.*)

DOK 3

At the clinic,

a nurse gives Lila a shot.

She feels better when

she gets a bandage.

141

READ FOR UNDERSTANDING

Make Connections

MODEL MAKING A CONNECTION

💬 **THINK ALOUD** *This reminds me of our school library. It has lots of bookshelves and places for people to look at books. I like to sit at a table and read books, just like Justin is doing in the photo.*

DOK 3

Places to Find Things

Justin bikes to the library

in his neighborhood.

He checks out books

about dinosaurs.

142

📖 **READ FOR UNDERSTANDING**

ASK: Where else could Jen and her dad get groceries? *(Possible responses: farmers' market, convenience store)*

FOLLOW-UP: What other places might be in their neighborhood? *(Accept reasonable responses.)*

DOK 2

📖 **READ FOR UNDERSTANDING**

Phonics/Decoding in Context

Have children point to the word *dad*. Review that when a word has a consonant followed by only one vowel, followed by a consonant, the vowel usually stands for its short vowel sound. **Model blending** the sounds in the word: /d/ /ă/ /d/, *dad*. Have children repeat.

Jen wants fruit and milk.

At the grocery store

her dad finds fresh grapefruit.

143

Neighborhoods can be big or small.

What places do you see in your neighborhood?

144

Turn and Talk

Places in My Neighborhood

Use details from **Places in My Neighborhood** to answer these questions with a partner.

1. **Make Connections** How are the neighborhoods in this text like the neighborhoods in **On the Map**?

2. How do neighborhood workers help people?

Talking Tip

Say your ideas. Be loud enough so that your partner can hear you.

I think that _____.

Academic Discussion

Use the TURN AND TALK routine. Remind children to share their ideas in a voice that is not too loud and not too soft and at a rate that is not too fast and not too slow.

Possible responses:

1. *There are town and city neighborhoods in both texts. Both texts show neighborhoods with different places where people live and work.* DOK 3

2. *Firefighters put out fires, police officers protect people, and nurses help people stay healthy.* DOK 2

145

Write a Description

PROMPT Choose a place from **Places in My Neighborhood**. What is this place like? Use the photos and sentences for ideas.

PLAN First, write words to describe the place. Tell what you can see and hear there.

Place:

WRITE Now write sentences to describe what this place is like. Remember to:

- Use describing words.
- Add details from the photos and sentences.

Responses may
vary.

Write About Reading

- **Read aloud** the Write section.
- **Encourage children** to add details from the photos and sentences, including describing words, that tell about sights and sounds in the place they are writing about.

DOK 3

147

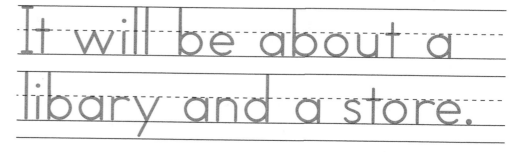

Independent Close Reading

Have children close read and annotate "What Is This Place?" on their own during small-group or independent work time. **As needed, use the Scaffolded Support** notes that follow to guide children who need additional help.

Scaffolded Support

As needed, remind children to:

- think about anything in this text that reminds them of something that happened to them, something they read about in another text or something that happened in society.

- figure out the meaning of social studies words and phrases by asking themselves questions about them and using context clues from both the text and the pictures to answer them.

DOK 2

Prepare to Read

GENRE STUDY **Informational text** is nonfiction. It gives facts about a topic.

MAKE A PREDICTION Preview **What Is This Place?** It has riddles about places in a community. What places do you think it will be about?

It will be about a
libary and a store.

SET A PURPOSE Read the clues to figure out the riddles about places in a community. Find out if your prediction is right.

What Is This Place?

READ What are some places in a community? <u>Underline</u> them.

This place is in a community.
Neighbors find books at this place.
    What is it?   A library!

You can go to this place on a bus.
Classmates go to this place.
    What is it?   A school!

Close Reading Tip

Circle words you don't know. Then figure them out.

CHECK MY UNDERSTANDING

Which words help you understand what a **library** is?

community, neighbors, books, place

Scaffolded Support

As needed, remind children to:

• pause to ask themselves questions about words or ideas they do not understand.

• look for clues in the text and pictures to figure out the meaning of new words.

DOK 2

149

READ <u>Underline</u> the places that this part tells about. Tell about times that you have been to places like these.

This place has signs.
You go to this place with money.
You go to this place to buy and sell.
  What is it?   A market!

Your mom and dad go with you.
A nurse helps you in this place.
  What is it?   A clinic!

CHECK MY UNDERSTANDING

Which words and picture details help you understand what a **market** is?

place, signs, money, buy, sell; food for people to buy

150

WRITE ABOUT IT Think about the pictures and information in **Places in My Neighborhood** and **What Is This Place?** Write about ways that the texts are alike. Then write how they are different.

Both have photos. Both tell about places in neighborhoods. One has sentences with information, but the other has riddles.

Scaffolded Support

As needed, guide children to:

• review both texts before they begin writing and make notes about the things that are the same and different. Have them use their notes to help them answer the question.

DOK 3

151

Prepare to Read

GENRE STUDY ▶ **Informational text** is nonfiction. It gives facts about a topic. Look for:

• facts about the world

• ways pictures and words give you information about the topic

SET A PURPOSE ▶ **Ask questions** before, during, and after you read to help you understand the text and get information. Look for evidence in the text and pictures to **answer** your questions.

POWER WORDS
spoon
against
churn
drive
stock
heal

Meet Julie Paschkis.

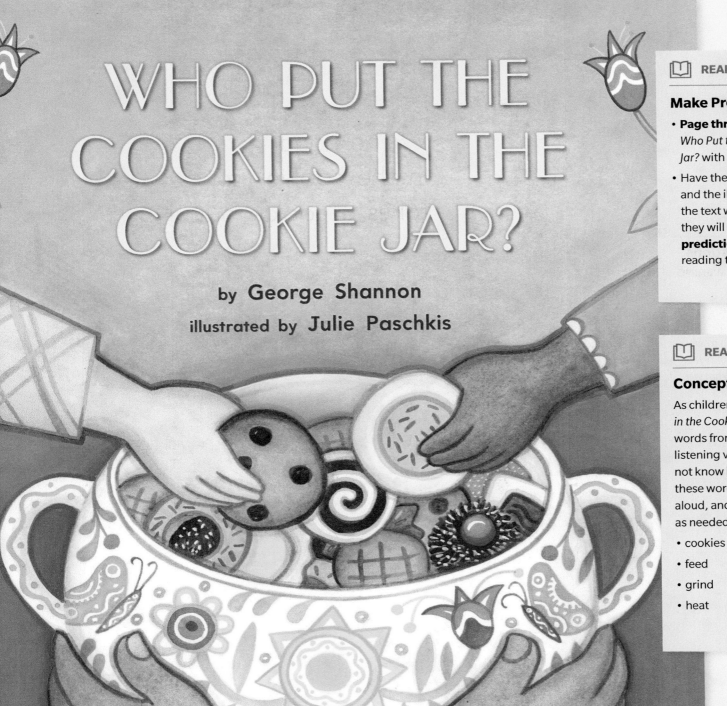

WHO PUT THE COOKIES IN THE COOKIE JAR?

by **George Shannon**

illustrated by **Julie Paschkis**

One hand
in the cookie jar
takes a cookie out.

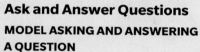

154

How many hands put the cookie **in**

is what the world's about.

155

 READ FOR UNDERSTANDING

Ask and Answer Questions

ASK: What questions did you have before you started reading this text? *(Responses will vary.)*

FOLLOW-UP: Have you been able to answer any of those questions? *How? (Accept reasonable responses.)*

DOK 2

 READ FOR UNDERSTANDING

ASK: What does the author mean when he says "how many hands put the cookie in"? *(that it takes more than one person to make a cookie)*

FOLLOW-UP: Why do you think the author made the word *in* red? *(to make sure the reader paid attention to it; so the reader compares it to the word out on the previous page)*

ANNOTATION TIP: Have children circle the words *in* and *out* on pages 154–155.

DOK 2

Hands that mix and stir the dough.

READ FOR UNDERSTANDING

ASK: Whose "hands" are making these cookies? *(a girl and her mom)*

FOLLOW-UP: What do you think they will do next? *(They will put the cookies in the oven to bake.)*

ANNOTATION TIP: Have children draw a line from the words "mix and stir" and "spoon" to the people in the illustration who are doing those things.

DOK 2

Spoon the clumps into a row.

156

Hands that make the cookie sheet.

📖 **READ FOR UNDERSTANDING**

Ask and Answer Questions

ASK: What questions might you ask about this part of the text? (*Possible responses: What part of making cookies is this about? How are these things used to make cookies?*)

FOLLOW-UP: How can you answer your questions? (*I can keep reading; I can look for details in the text and pictures.*)

DOK 2

Oven mitts against the heat.

157

and milk the cow.

Churn the butter.

Guide the plow.

📖 **READ FOR UNDERSTANDING**

ASK: How do we get butter? *(It's made from stirring milk.)*

FOLLOW-UP: What evidence tells you this? *(The text says "milk the cow" and "churn the butter." The picture shows a man holding a bucket of milk. He is helping a girl churn it into butter.)*

ANNOTATION TIP: Have children circle the details in the illustration that help them answer the question.

DOK 2

📖 **READ FOR UNDERSTANDING**

Ask and Answer Questions

MODEL ASKING AND ANSWERING A QUESTION

🔍 **THINK ALOUD** *While I read the text, I think of questions I have about it. I use question words such as who, what, where, when, why, or how. For example, I might ask myself: Why is the woman plowing the field? Then I look for evidence or keep reading to answer my question.*

DOK 2

Hands that sow
and grind the wheat

 READ FOR UNDERSTANDING

Phonics/Decoding in Context

Have children point to the word *us*. Review that when a word has only one vowel followed by a consonant, the vowel usually stands for its short vowel sound. **Model blending** the sounds in the word: /ŭ/ /s/, *us*. Have children repeat.

 READ FOR UNDERSTANDING

Ask and Answer Questions
MODEL ASKING AND ANSWERING A QUESTION

🗨 **THINK ALOUD** *While I was reading the previous page, I asked myself why the woman was plowing the field. On this page, I see a man throwing seeds, and the text says someone is sowing, or planting seeds. I think the woman was plowing a field to plant wheat on it. I was able to answer my question when I kept reading.*

DOK 2

into flour for us to eat.

160

Hands that tend and feed the hens.

Gather eggs. Build the pens.

161

**Phonics/Decoding
in Context**

Have children point to the word *Cut*.
Review that when a consonant is
followed by a vowel, and that vowel is
followed by another consonant, the
vowel usually stands for its short
vowel sound. **Model blending** the
sounds in the word: /k/ /ŭ/ /t/, *cut*.
Have children repeat.

Hands that harvest sugarcane.
Cut and grind.
Load the train.

162

163

Hands that load the trucks and drive.

📖 **READ FOR UNDERSTANDING**

ASK: How do truck drivers help make cookies? *(They take the ingredients from the places where they are made to the places where people can buy them.)*

DOK 2

164

Stock the shelves when things arrive.

📖 **READ FOR UNDERSTANDING**

ASK: What are the people stocking the shelves with? *(milk, butter, flour, eggs, and sugar)*

FOLLOW-UP: How do you know? *(Possible responses: Those are the ingredients from the previous pages; that is what I see in the picture.)*

ANNOTATION TIP: Guide children to label the different ingredients in the illustration.

DOK 2

165

Hands that clothe and feed them all.
Heal and teach.
Large and small.

166

Hands that help
the hands that help
are what the world's about . . .

167

. . . **many** put
the cookie in,

so **one** can
take it out.

📖 READ FOR UNDERSTANDING

ASK: Why do you think the author made the words on this page a different color? *(Possible responses: to let the reader know that these words are important; to remind the reader of the beginning of the text)*

FOLLOW-UP: How are these two words related? *(They have opposite meanings.)*

ANNOTATION TIP: Have children underline the words *many* and *one*.

DOK 2

168

SUGAR COOKIES

1 cup sugar
½ cup unsalted butter, melted
1 egg
2 tablespoons milk
2 teaspoons vanilla
1 ½ cups all-purpose flour
½ teaspoon baking powder
½ teaspoon salt

- Preheat oven to 375 degrees.

- Grease 2 cookie sheets.

- Combine sugar, melted butter, egg, milk, and vanilla. Beat or stir until smooth.

- In a small bowl, combine flour, baking powder, and salt.

- Add the flour mixture to the sugar mixture and beat or stir until combined.

- Drop teaspoons of dough onto a cookie sheet, and press each cookie down with the bottom of a glass or the palm of your hand.

- Bake 10 to 12 minutes at 375 degrees, until the edges just begin to turn golden brown. Cool for 2 minutes on the cookie sheets, then transfer to cooling racks.

Makes about 3 dozen cookies.

170

Turn and Talk

Use details from **Who Put the Cookies in the Cookie Jar?** to answer these questions with a partner.

1. **Ask and Answer Questions** What questions did you have before, during, and after reading the text? How did the questions help you understand the information?

2. What jobs do people do to help make cookies?

Talking Tip

Use this sentence to add your own idea to what your partner says.

My idea is _____.

171

READ Together

Write a Thank-You Note

PROMPT Choose a worker to thank from **Who Put the Cookies in the Cookie Jar?** Why do you think the person is helpful?

PLAN First, draw a picture of the person. Show what they do to help make the cookies.

Write About Reading

- **Read aloud** the prompt.
- **Lead a discussion** in which children identify the workers and what they do. Ask them to share their ideas about how the workers are helpful. Tell them to use text evidence to support their ideas.
- Then read aloud the Plan section. Have children use ideas from the discussion in their drawings.

DOK 3

WRITE Now write a note to thank the person. Tell why what they do helps make the cookies. Remember to:

- Write the word **I** with a capital letter.

- Sign your name. Begin it with a capital letter.

Responses may vary.

Write About Reading

- **Read aloud** the Write section.

- **Encourage children** to include details that tell why being able to make and eat cookies is important to them. Have children write the pronoun *I* and their names with a capital letter.

DOK 3

173

Independent Close Reading

Have children close read and annotate "Kids Can Help" on their own during small-group or independent work time. As needed, **use the Scaffolded Support notes** that follow to guide children who need additional help.

Scaffolded Support

As needed, remind children to:

- ask and answer questions before, during, and after they read to help them understand the text.

- look for how the text is organized, and think about how it helps them understand the text.

DOK 3

Prepare to Read

GENRE STUDY ▶ **Informational text** is nonfiction. It gives facts about a topic.

MAKE A PREDICTION ▶ Preview **Kids Can Help**. It tells how kids can help make cookies. What do you think you will learn about?

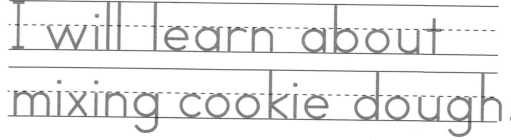

I will learn about mixing cookie dough.

SET A PURPOSE ▶ Ask yourself questions before, during, and after you read to help yourself understand the different jobs kids can do to help.

174

Kids Can Help

Scaffolded Support

As needed, remind children that:

- authors sometimes organize their texts by describing things one after another.

- they can look for action words to help them understand each job.

- they should ask themselves questions before, during, and after reading to make sure they understand the text.

DOK 2

READ <u>Underline</u> the jobs kids can do to help make cookies.

Who wants to help make cookies?
Kids can do many jobs to help.
Kids can get the spoons and pans.
Kids can mix with the spoons.
Kids can not do one job.
Mom will put the pan in. ▶

Close Reading Tip

Put a ? by the parts you have questions about.

CHECK MY UNDERSTANDING

Describe one of the jobs kids can do.

Kids mix the cookie
dough with a spoon.

175

READ <u>Underline</u> the jobs kids can do to help clean up.

Can kids help with the mess?
Yes! Kids can get the mop and mop up the room.
Kids can find the spoons.
But kids can not take the hot cookies out.
Dad will do this job.
Kids can do one last job.
Kids can enjoy the cookies! Yum!

CHECK MY UNDERSTANDING

Write a question you still have about **Kids Can Help**.

What did the kids mix together to make the cookie dough?

176

WRITE ABOUT IT The author describes different jobs in **Kids Can Help**. What are some jobs kids can do? Why is describing one job after another a good way for the author to give the information?

Kids can mix the dough. They can mop. It is good to find out what kids can do first to make the cookies and then later to clean up.

Scaffolded Support

As needed, guide children to name jobs kids can do and then include details about how they do those jobs.

DOK 2

177

📖 VIEW FOR UNDERSTANDING

Introduce the Video

• **Read aloud** and discuss the information about the genre.

• **Guide children** to set a purpose for viewing to practice using context clues to determine the meaning of content-area words.

• Provide information about the background topic, Interesting Jobs.

Prepare to View

GENRE STUDY **Videos** are short movies. Some videos give information. Others are for you to watch for enjoyment. Watch and listen for:

• the purpose of the video

• information about the topic

• the language and the words used

SET A PURPOSE Find out about jobs. Listen for new words about jobs. Use clues in the sentences you hear and the pictures to help you understand the meanings of the words.

Build Background: Interesting Jobs

178

Curious About Jobs

📖 **VIEW FOR UNDERSTANDING**

Make Predictions

• **Display** the cover of *Curious About Jobs* for children.

• Have them **use prior knowledge** and the opening picture to predict what the video will be about. Tell children they will **return to their predictions** after they finish watching the video.

DOK 2

As You View Listen for special words like **mechanic**, **potter**, and **museum**. They tell about certain jobs. Use the sentences the children say and the pictures to help you understand what these special words mean.

📖 VIEW FOR UNDERSTANDING

Content-Area Words

ASK: Which questions could you ask yourself if you did not know the meaning of the word *mechanic*? *(Possible response: Which clues from the text can I use to figure it out?)*

FOLLOW-UP: How would you answer your question? *(The video shows a man using tools to work on an airplane. The audio says that the mechanic pokes inside the engine, checks the wires and oil, tightens screws, and makes the airplane safe.)*

DOK 2

180

Curious About Jobs

Use details from **Curious About Jobs** to answer these questions with a partner.

1. **Content-Area Words** How does each worker do his or her job? Use some new words you learned to help you explain.

2. Which job is most interesting to you? Use details from the video to tell why.

Talking Tip

Say your ideas. Speak clearly and not too fast or too slow.

I think that _____.

Academic Discussion

Use the TURN AND TALK routine.
Remind children to use complete sentences when they share their ideas and to speak clearly and at an appropriate rate so their partners can understand them.

Possible responses:

1. *Accept reasonable responses.* DOK 2

2. *Responses will vary.* DOK 3

181

READ
Together

Let's Wrap Up!

(?) Essential Question

How does everyone in my family and community make it special?

Pick one of these activities to show what you have learned about the topic.

1. Act It Out

Choose one of the community places you have read about. Work with a partner. Act out things you can do in that place. Can your other classmates guess the place?

182

2. Award Time

You have read about special people in families and in the community. Who deserves an award? Make the award. Then write sentences. Tell why the person deserves it.

Word Challenge

Can you use the word working in your sentences?

Award Time
- **Guide children** to revisit the texts they read and think about why each person might deserve an award.
- **Encourage them** to use the Big Idea Word *working* as they explain their opinions.

DOK 3

My Notes

Brainstorm and Plan

Have children use the My Notes space to jot down ideas for their chosen activity. Remind them to refer back to their notes as they complete the activity.

183

Glossary

A

against If one thing is used **against** another, it keeps something from being harmed.
Wear a coat to stay warm **against** the cold.

area An **area** is a part of a bigger place.
My class has a special **area** to play in at school.

area

B

beautiful Something that is **beautiful** is nice to look at.
The flowers are **beautiful** colors.

beautiful

184

C

challenge A **challenge** is something that is hard to do.
Running up a big hill is a **challenge**.

changed If something **changed**, it became different from what it was.
The caterpillar **changed** into a butterfly!

chilly When something is **chilly**, it is cold.
Put on a coat if you are **chilly**.

churn When you **churn** something, you stir it quickly for a long time.
Churn the cream until it turns into butter.

chilly

churn

185

clinic

clinic   A **clinic** is a place where people go to see a doctor or nurse.
Did you go to a **clinic** when you cut your foot?

community   A **community** is made up of people who live near each other and the places around them.
We all went to see the parade in our **community**.

D

drive   When you **drive** something, you make it go where you want it to go.
The racers **drive** their cars around the track.

drive

E

emotions   Emotions are strong feelings we have, like happiness or sadness.
We feel happy **emotions** when our team wins.

enjoy   If you **enjoy** doing something, you really like it.
We **enjoy** watching movies.

excited   When you feel **excited**, you are very happy.
The **excited** children cheered when they got their prizes.

excited

F

friendship   When you have a **friendship** with someone, you like the person.
Our nice **friendship** started the day we met.

friendship

187

G

great   Something that is **great** is better than good.
We love to eat the **great** food Mom makes.

H

heal

heal   When doctors **heal** sick or hurt people, they help them get well.
She put a bandage on my hand to **heal** it.

help   When you **help**, you make it easier for someone to do something.
I **help** my dad do the dishes.

help

K

kinds   If there are many **kinds** of something, there are many different groups of it.
We saw all **kinds** of animals at the zoo.

188

L

last   When something happens at **last**, it happens after a long time.
We waited, and the school bus came at **last**.

M

map   A **map** is a picture that shows streets, rivers, and other parts of a place.
I can find many places on the **map**.

map

market   A **market** is a place where people can buy things.
We go to the **market** to buy food.

mess   If something is a **mess**, it is not neat.
I cleaned up the **mess** in my room.

market

189

N

neighbors

neighbors   Your **neighbors** are the people who live near you.
We talk to the **neighbors** we see next door.

nervous   When you feel **nervous**, you are worried about what might happen.
I was **nervous** the first time I tried to ride a bike.

new   When something is **new**, you have never seen, had, or done it before.
I am going to a **new** school this year.

P

paddled

paddled   If you **paddled** through water, you swam by moving your hands and feet.
He jumped in the pool and **paddled** to the side.

partner   A **partner** is someone you work with or play with.

My **partner** and I make something together.

places   **Places** are certain parts of a city or town.

Does your town have **places** to ride bikes?

population   The **population** is the number of people who live in a place.

The crowded city has a big **population**.

purpose   A **purpose** is a reason for doing or having something.

The **purpose** of the sign is to tell drivers to stop.

partner

population

191

S

sell

spoon

sell   When you **sell** something, you give it to someone who gives you money for it.
I get some money when I **sell** things.

set   When you **set** something up, you make it so that it is useful.
Let's **set** up tables for the party.

spoon   When you **spoon** food, you pick it up with a spoon.
Spoon the food into the baby's mouth.

stock   When you **stock** something, you fill it up with things.
Stock the empty shelf with cans of food.

192

T

together   When friends do things **together**, they do them with each other.
The friends play a game **together**.

town   A **town** is a place where people live that is smaller than a city.
We know most of the people in our small **town**.

town

trip   When you go on a **trip**, you go from one place to another.
My family took a **trip** to the lake.

try   When you **try** to do something, you work at doing it.
Every day, I **try** to learn to ride my bike.

try

193

U

ugly   If something is **ugly**, it is not nice to look at.

I like green, but my friend thinks it is **ugly**.

W

wished

wished   If you **wished** for something, you wanted it to happen.

I **wished** for a new game for my birthday.

working

working   If you are **working**, you are doing a job.

They are **working** to build a car.

194

Index of Titles and Authors

Acknowledgments

Excerpt from *First Girl Scout* by Ginger Wadsworth. Text copyright © 2012 by Clarion Books, an imprint of Houghton Mifflin Harcourt. Reprinted by permission of Houghton Mifflin Harcourt Publishing Company.

Places in My Neighborhood by Shelly Lyons. Text copyright © 2013 by Capstone Press, a Capstone imprint. Reprinted by permission of Capstone Press Publishers.

Who Put the Cookies in the Cookie Jar? by George Shannon, illustrated by Julie Paschkis. Text copyright © 2013 by George Shannon. Illustrations copyright © 2013 by Julie Paschkis. Reprinted by arrangement with Henry Holt Books for Young Readers, and by permission of Sheldon Fogelman and Wernick & Pratt Agency.

Credits

4 (top girl) ©suzieleakey/iStock/Getty Images, (top bg) ©ayelet-keshet/Shutterstock; 5 (t) ©Lise Gagne/E+/Getty Images; 6 (top soccer boy) ©BJI/Blue Jean Images/Getty Images, (top reading boy) ©Scholastic Studio 10/Photolibrary/Getty Images, (top girl) ©Kalmatsuy/Shutterstock, (top standing boy) ©drbimages/iStock/Getty Images Plus; 7 (t) ©Tom Fawls/Dreamstime, (b Curious About Jobs) ©Clarion Books/Houghton Mifflin Company; 8 (bg) ©Dan Sedran/Shutterstock, (l) ©kaloriya/Fotolia, (r) ©mimagephotography/iStockPhoto.com; 9 ©sutham/Shutterstock; 12 (r) ©suzieleakey/Getty Images, (bg) ©ayelet-keshet/Shutterstock; 14 ©Sean Masterson; 16 (tl) ©GS/Gallery Stock Limited, (tr) ©Add New Photographer/Dreamstime, (bl) ©JGI/Jamie Grill/Media Bakery, (br) ©Monkey Business Images/Dreamstime; 20 ©GS/Gallery Stock Limited; 22 ©FatCamera/iStockPhoto.com; 24 (tr) ©FatCamera/iStockPhoto.com, (bl) ©asiseeit/iStockPhoto.com; 32 ©Elisa Chavarri; 50 ©PeopleImages/iStockPhoto.com; 51 (bg) ©Lise Gagne/E+/Getty Images, (c) ©WhitePlaid/Shutterstock, (b) ©GlobalStock/Vetta/Getty Images, (t) ©paulaphoto/Shutterstock; 52 ©kali9/E+/Getty Images; 53 (tl) ©Pressmaster/Shutterstock, (tr) ©Huntstock/Getty Images, (cl) ©Amble Design/Shutterstock, (cr) ©Hero Images/Digital Vision/Getty Images, (bl) ©Monkey Business Images/Shutterstock, (br) ©WhitePlaid/Shutterstock; 54 ©dbimages/Alamy; 55 (tl) ©GlobalStock/Vetta/Getty Images, (tr), (bl) ©Hero Images/Alamy, (cl) ©Pressmaster/Shutterstock, (cr) ©MBI/Alamy, (br) ©Jurgen Magg/Alamy; 56 ©Monkey Business Images/Shutterstock; 57 ©Alinute Silzeviciute/Shutterstock; 58 ©szefei/iStockPhoto.com; 59 (tl) ©Amble Design/Shutterstock, (tr) ©kali9/E+/Getty Images, (cl) ©Image Source Trading Ltd/Shutterstock, (cr) ©implementarfilms/Fotolia, (bl) ©MN Studio/Shutterstock, (br) ©Media Photos/iStockPhoto.com; 60 ©paulaphoto/Shutterstock; 68 ©Gail Carson Levine; 86 ©The Fuzees; 87–88 *Video still from I'm Me* ©The FuZees; 90 ©OIScher/Shutterstock; 91 (r) ©yasinguneysu/iStockPhoto.com, (l) ©Rawpixel.com/Shutterstock; 96 (l) ©BJI/Blue Jean Images/Getty Images, (tr) ©Scholastic Studio 10/Photolibrary/Getty Images, (br) ©snake3d/iStock/Getty Images Plus/Getty Images; 97 (l) ©Kalmatsuy/Shutterstock, (r) ©drbimages/iStock/Getty Images Plus; 98 ©Wong Herbert Yee; 120 ©dibrova/Shutterstock; 122 ©JamesBrey/iStockPhoto.com; 124 ©6381380/iStockPhoto.com; 126 (t) ©Craig Tuttle/Design Pics/Getty Images, (b) ©Filtv/Dreamstime, (r) ©Kleber Cordeiro costa/Alamy; 134 ©imantsu/iStockPhoto.com; 135 ©Tom Fawls/Dreamstime; 136 ©JayLazarin/iStock/Getty Images; 137 ©trekandshoot/Shutterstock; 138 ©DNY59/E+/Getty Images; 139 ©Capstone Studio/Karon Dubke; 140 ©Capstone Studio/Karon Dubke; 141 ©Capstone Studio/Karon Dubke; 142 ©phi2/iStockPhoto.com; 143, 144 ©Capstone Studio/Karon Dubke; 148 (l) ©SelectStock/iStockPhoto.com, (r) ©Ceri Breeze/Shutterstock, (t) ©umiberry/Shutterstock; 149 (l) ©Tyler Olson/Shutterstock, (r) ©Monkey Business Images/Shutterstock; 150 ©Ceri Breeze/Shutterstock; 152 ©Joe Max Emminger; 178 ©inhauscreative/iStockPhoto.com; 179–180 *Video still from Curious About Jobs* ©Clarion Books/Houghton Mifflin Company; 182 ©Apple's Eyes Studio/Shutterstock; 183 ©Igor Kisselev/Getty Images; 184 (t) ©art nick/Shutterstock, (b) ©Medioimages/Photodisc/Getty Images; 185 (t) ©Blue Jean Images/Getty Images, (b) ©Frances Benjamin Johnston Collection/Library of Congress Prints & Photographs Division; 186 (t) ©Wavebreak Premium/Shutterstock, (b) ©Nicola Gavin/Alamy; 187 (t) ©Amble Design/Shutterstock, (b) ©Photodisc/Getty Images; 188 (t) ©SelectStock/Vetta/Getty Images; 189 (t) ©Monalyn Gracia/Corbis; 190 (t) ©Golden Pixels LLC/Shutterstock, (b) ©Sami Sarkis/Alamy Images; 191 (b) ©blvdone/Shutterstock; 192 (b) ©YakobchukOlena/Shutterstock; 193 (t) ©Sean Pavone/Shutterstock, (b) ©Photodisc/Getty Images; 194 (t) ©Ryan McVay/Photodisc/Getty Images, (b) ©Vasily Smirnov/Fotolia